Fly Girl Etiquette

A Modern Guide to Manners
And
A Properly Fabulous Life

PHIRE D. COLE

CONTENTS

Foreword

As a child of the American nineteen sixties, an adolescent of the seventies and a teenager of the eighties, I walked right into the fly era. I was a curious and daring black boy, growing up in inner-city Philadelphia, who paid strict attention to all of the details. And in the nineteen eighties, the details were everywhere. That's what being "fly" was all about. We wanted to stand out and elevate above all others with our attention-getting style, our bold attitudes and our individual flavor. Through creation of break dancing, pop locking, graffiti, rapping and spinning records at block parties, recreational centers, playgrounds and public parks, we became the most celebrated teenagers America had ever produced. In fact, our creation of hip hop music and culture is still ongoing and worldwide.

Right smack in the middle of 1985—the year of my sweet sixteen birthday—a rap group called the Boogie Boys out of Brooklyn, New York released the song that would change my life forever. *Flyy Girls*, all about the inner-city girls of New York, New Jersey, Philly, Boston, DC, Baltimore and more, who exemplified what it meant to present yourself to world as valuable and worth every penny. That's where I got the double yy spelling from. The Boogie Boys emphasized it— *"A flyyyyyyy girl..."*

You can call it superficial if you want, but when a fifteen-year-old girl left her house in the nineteen eighties in a two-toned, asymmetric hairstyle, with gold jewelry around her neck and wrists, in designer sunglasses, blue jeans, skirts, shoes and a Gucci bag to carry her make-up, lotion and lip gloss in, you knew that she meant *business*. And we took these fly girls seriously, because they took themselves seriously.

It meant a lot for a young, inner-city girl to feel that comfortable and confident in herself to go all out and put us guys on notice. "Do not step to me unless you got enough game to handle me." And I didn't have enough game. So I buckled down in my college years and wrote a whole book about it, a *Flyy Girl* book that became legendary for inner-city girls who rarely had heroes, especially not in a book. I went on to create a *Flyy Girl* logo, a fashion and lifestyle magazine, sold *Fly Girl* tank tops and produced a theme song back in 2005.

However, now that we're thirty years removed from the nineteen eighties, the word "fly" is barely even used anymore—particularly not by young women. Guys tend to use the word more, while they continue to present themselves with more jewelry, earrings, fashion, style, attitude and flavor than most girls do. The young girls like to use the word "hot" now, which seems much smaller, insignificant and temporary.

A *Flyy Girl* from my era would spend a whole *hour* getting herself ready for school, the movies, a trip to the mall, the playground and definitely for a party. But a "hot girl" seems to be much less stunning or impactful. She's a simple head nod, where a fly girl was a complete stare down. Metaphorically, we looked at fly girls as well-cooked dish at a steak and potatoes restaurant, who forced us to do more, where a hot girl is more a quick McDonald's takeout meal.

Maybe I'm just too old to understand the trends of this new era, but when I think of the flyness of the past and the sisters who stood out for their style, flavor, ambition, dress code and overall presence, Dianne Carroll, Cicely Tyson, Pam Grier, Eartha Kitt, Beverly Johnson and Jackie Kennedy come to mind. But how many young girls of year 2015 have ever even heard of those sisters? I guess I'd be better off referencing Mary J. Blige and Jennifer Lopez now as old-school *Flyy Girls* who still spend the time to think about how they present themselves to the world as womanly, established, respectable and still valuable sisters who enjoy pulling stylish clothes on instead spending so much time taking them off or barely wearing any. And who will ever forget the individual style and flavor of Aaliyah? She was a young, talented, highly respected and fashionable sister who was super-duper fly, as multi-talented writer and producer Missy Elliott once rapped.

I continue to reflect on the holistic idea of African kings and queens, who urban community leaders loved to link us to for aspiration pursuits. And kings and queens of every culture were people who dressed *up* and never down. "Dressing up" tends to provide one with the perception of higher expectations of their character and goals, like the urban church girls who wear elaborate dresses, stockings, gloves and hats on each and every Sunday. Or the superstar divas of every race, hue and nationality who stand out and receive notice at award shows. Every day was an award show for the nineteen eighties *Fly Girl*. I miss that era, along with the higher challenge that a true *Fly Girl* used to present to a guy.

So when Phire Dawson approached me about this idea of publishing a *Fly Girl Etiquette* book to reestablish the meaning of fly for the young women of this new era, I told Phire, "Let's just make sure we get it right."

Nevertheless, I do understand that people, ideas and culture are forever changing. With those changes in mind, I figured it would be cool and fun to mix my old-school, masculine perspective with Phire's new school woman approach and see what we could come up a new fly—thirty years later—for the inner-city, suburban and international girls of 2015.

Omar Tyree

Introduction

Let me begin by telling you what this book is not. Close the cover and put the book back on the shelf if you think you are going to get an old school etiquette Emily Post speech. I love the guides and information from Ms. Post, but *Fly Girl Etiquette* is far from preaching to you about being a submissive woman in 1897. . . That's the year Emily Post, the famous manners coach, was twenty-five years old. Times have changed! Women have changed. Instead, I want to continue what Ophelia DeVore started. Etiquette and poise with power. DeVore was a formal model and etiquette coach who trained the great and beautiful women we love. Diahann Carroll, Cicely Tyson, Eartha Kitt, and famous model, Helen Williams. These well-known women were trained to be dynamic, poised, and beautiful. They had more than looks to offer the world. These classic beauties and many women who carry a similar attitude today are called fly.

Some of us still carry the essence of being fly, but we have become too busy to focus on our personal standards and etiquette. The women of today fight on the front lines with men, we are single mothers, and date several men before getting married. If you are anything like me, you also like the occasional pole dancing class and after party drink.

Fly Girl Etiquette is about loving yourself and being the best person you can be in today's world. You can be a lady *and* do a striptease in your bedroom for your man. You can balance your checking account *and* splurge on an expensive pair of shoes. You can also choose to never marry *and* take advantage of being the single Fly Girl in town. Our grandmothers could never fathom what today's world is like, so why would we live by their old standards.

It is the age of reality television where being outrageous or releasing a sex tape can make you famous. In today's world, the majority of women go to college, they manage their own finances, spend much of their time at work and with friends, have casual sexual encounters (online or in person), purchase their own homes, party all night, *and* will defend their right to do so. The old rules do not apply anymore. We have it all!

I can imagine your eyes rolling, and you might think, *If I have it all, why do I need this book?* Frankly, we do have it all, but our manners and etiquette are in the toilet, along with the 1897 etiquette rules.

Even if we look back 30 or 40 years ago to Diana Ross and Eartha Kitt, walking in a room was a presentation of elegance. Have we ever seen any footage of Cicely Tyson or Jackie Kennedy throwing a drink in a person's face, often aired on reality show cat fights... NO! I work in Hollywood every day and I ask myself, "why be a self-respecting lady when we see people making money and getting attention by selling their intimate stories with celebrities, releasing a sex tape, or fighting in the street?" Our personal well-being has slipped out of our grasp, putting unworthy men and work before our own needs and causing us to forget about our own value.

We have the extra task of monitoring our lives and the people around us in a way that our mothers never had to. We struggle to keep our private lives private as our social media involvement explodes on Facebook, Instagram, and networking sites soon to come. We are losing jobs, losing great boyfriends, and forsaking friends because of our behavior.

I'm here to help you have it all without losing self-respect and lowering your standards. A fly girl with etiquette knows she has it all and improves her life with her skills.

I've included tried and tested lifestyle etiquette, manners, and helpful tips on looking great, feeling great, and always thinking in progressive and insightful ways. Fly girls like Angela Basset, Lupita Nyong'o, and Kerry

Washington appear to live by these etiquette rules and techniques on television and in everyday life.

I want to share with you my etiquette techniques, which I learned from my experiences. I've practiced these same rules when modeling on *The Price Is Right*, dancing for the NFL's Atlanta Falcons, performing in pageants, and networking for my life and career. You will learn how to walk into a room and command attention. You will learn how to look sexy and sultry in bed, or with a simple dance move. You will learn how to hold an in-depth and well-informed conversation with anyone who crosses your path.

You will feel confident, sexier, and more carefree after I share what I've learned from working in front of and behind the camera. You will become a fly girl with etiquette.

I feel so passionate about helping you because I was once the shy girl. I was overlooked and lacked confidence. Money was not plentiful in my home. I never had formal etiquette training. I will be the first to tell you money does not equal etiquette or personal value and self-love. Everything you will read on these pages is through personal training and trial and error.

I was a skinny, stuttering, pimple-faced teen who found a way to be my best with what I was given. I am barely five feet five inches, weigh 110 pounds, and work as a model. People are surprised to know I was in speech class until age sixteen and continue etiquette training and speech classes today. I say this to emphasize that being a fly girl with etiquette has nothing to do with physical beauty or trying to be perfect. This is about *you* having personal standards for yourself.

I came to a conclusion that I am the person that I am because I was taught by my parents to love and respect myself. I was taught to treat others with respect, whether I knew them or not. I had to be my best self when faced with adversities.

Fly Girl Etiquette wants you to live a fabulous and carefree life without being careless.

1

"I don't dress for other people's opinion. I dress for my own opinion." – Kerry Washington

Personal Appearance

I became an NFL cheerleader at 19 years old. I was in college and very excited to achieve my lifelong goal of cheering for a professional team. Like many college students, my finances were little to none. I couldn't afford to buy the proper auditioning attire. Instead, I auditioned in a swimsuit, not a leotard. I cleaned some old sneakers and brushed some makeup on my face to look a little sexier and more mature

I was ready for the big crowds, the grueling practices, and the many appearances. Once I made it to the team, however, my new cheerleading thought otherwise. My coach and the director pulled me into a private room and picked my looks apart. As I sat on the carpeted floor, the two women sat on chairs before me, legs crossed, staring at me and writing on their notepads.

"Your hair needs color and highlights to frame your face."

"Your skin needs a lot a work. Clear up the acne."

"Whiten your teeth."

As the list was read, I felt embarrassed and sick. I was not hurt; I was pained because my coach was right. Her reputation was on the line, and her job was to make sure I looked my best and complemented the other women on the team.

I was a woman at 19 and had failed to make sure I looked my best at all times. Truth be told, my minor imperfections could have cost me my dream, but instead, a mirror was held before my face, and I was told to do better, and I did. I added highlights and learned more about the tones of highlights that complement my complexion. I whitened my teeth. I was put on medication to treat the severe acne. By the time the season's first game was scheduled, I was the woman I thought I should be at 19. I looked my best, and I felt great. From that point on I paid close attention to my physical appearance and how it translates to the rest of the world.

How to Dress

When deciding on the proper attire to wear, you must always think about your day's events or what occasion you will be attending. If you are going to attend classes and walk from building to building, sit at a coffee shop, or hang out with friends, casual clothes will be appropriate. Cocktail parties, weddings, and special dates will need clothes made for special occasions: gowns, cocktail dresses, or dressy slacks and blouses. And of course, business attire, such as tailored suits and high-cut blouses, should be worn to achieve a professional look. Look in your closet and make sure you have all the items you need for any event, whether large or small. Below is a list of essential items in every woman's closet:

Key Clothing Basics
Basic black suit (pants, skirt, and a two- to three-button jacket)
Black sheath dress
White classic collared dress shirt
Jeans (darker-rinse that fits your body well)
Black pumps
All-weather trench coat in tan, navy blue, or black
Clean casual sneakers
Several white basic T-shirts that fit your body well (shirts with 1 or 2

percent spandex have a great fit)

Casual cotton slacks or chinos

Party top that can dress up jeans, slacks, or a skirt

Diamond or cubic zirconia studs (the bright clear rocks frame your smile, making your teeth look whiter; diamond studs are classic and work with all outfits)

Closet Add-On's

- Day Dress
- Polished Tote Bag that can carry today's paper and pumps
- Swimsuit
- Sweatpants and Jacket Alternative: outfit great for flying and running errands
- Workout Sneakers
- Stylish Workout Clothes
- Lounge Clothes
- Evening Bag
- Sexy Heels you feel confident in
- Ballet Flats

Your *key clothing basics* should make it through any trend and current fad. You should buy quality key items. Update and add on your basics wardrobe when they become worn. Your *closet add-ons* can always be changed to work with the current trends.

Dress Your Body Type

Many of us have the key clothing items, but they are not the best fit for our body type. Get to know your body. Look at yourself in the mirror and be honest about your body shape. This will allow you to shop properly and feel great in your clothes.

Standard Body Types

A woman's body type varies depending on height, torso and limb lengths, and weight. Knowing your body helps you determine what clothing items look best on you and accentuates your most eye-catching parts.

Love You

Look at yourself in the mirror and in pictures. Divide your body into three areas: your head and neck, your upper body from shoulders to hips, and your lower body from hips to toes. Pick at least one part that you love about in each area. You can pick your eyes and your neck, your shoulders and your waist, and your knees and your toes, for example—it doesn't matter.

Pick parts of you that you love, and play with them. If you love your eyes, invest in the perfect mascara or eye shadows. If your favorite parts are your legs, wear shorts and skirts to show them off. The result will be you leaving the house every day loving your outfit as well as your body.

Let's Go Shopping

When I go shopping, I have one of two motivations: I want to window-shop or do add-on shopping (buying an extra item to complete an outfit I already have), or I *need* an item or an outfit for an event. I approach each motivation very differently.

When I am window-shopping or looking for something to add it my closet, I dress casually. I am ready to spend hours walking and looking for items that *catch* my attention.

I don't care what undergarments I am wearing, as long as I am comfortable. I rarely get assistance from the store staff because I am shopping based on a whim or an attraction.

During my *need*-based shopping, I wear or bring undergarments that match what I would wear with the item I am looking for (bring a strapless bra if you are looking for a strapless dress). I wear a little makeup so I can see the partially made-up me with the outfit on. I also wear a button-down top or dress that easily slides on and off so I can get in and out of my clothes without rubbing my makeup during quick changes. And the most important thing is *I ask for help*. I have a mental or written list of what I need. I go to the most fashionable sales associate I see. I tell him or her what I need exactly and whether I am open to any modifications and suggestions. This will make my shopping quick and direct. When you ask a sales associate for help, he or she will bring you what you are asking for or help you find everything you need.

Your Shopping List

Jeans

Many designers make all types of jeans for all body types, trends, fabrication blends, and budgets. Every woman can find a pair of jeans that works for her. Be honest with yourself about your body and your shape and wear jeans that fit you. Pick a day that you are not bloated so your body and mind are comfortable with your shape. If you are not sure, spend a day visiting several stores, trying on jeans. Inform the salesperson that you are trying on jeans to find the best fit for your body. Ask the sales staff for suggestions and ideas on how you can wear the latest styles. You are *not* obligated to buy their items. By the end of the day, you should be familiar with which fabrics and cuts look good on you.

HINT: Informing the salesperson you are only trying on clothes in hopes of finding a good fit relieves the stress of listening to sales tactics and allows you to try, try, try in a relaxed environment.

Get a Great Fit

Jeans, like many other types of clothes, look good on you only when you take the time to find a pair that fits your body and achieves the look you desire. Denim jeans come in many styles: cropped, skinny, boot-cut, pipe, straight-leg, low-rise, high-waist, and flared. Once you decide on a style, you must check its fit. You should not have skin and fat (muffin top) hanging over the top of the jeans or pants. The length should fit the shoes or heels you plan to wear with the pants.

Dark-wash straight-leg or slight boot-cut jeans that are not skintight make you look slimmer. Solid dark-rinse jeans are great to wear with heels because they make you look taller. Dark denim jeans can also be dressed up and down.

Even though jeans are a casual look, you need to have them tailored to fit your body. Most clothes are purchased off-the-rack (mass-produced or not custom-made for you). Denim is not one size fits all, so hem the pant legs if the pants are too long, trim the waist if there is a gap between the waist and the waistband, etc.

Many jeans today are low-rise. We have all seen women who have their panties rising out, or worse, have their butt cheeks peeking out the top of their jeans. It is very tacky to show your "whale tail" or butt crack to the world. We ladies have several options if we like the low-rise look. We can wear a long shirt or purchase clothing options that hide the peek-a-boo bottom, purchase low-rise panties, "go commando" (no panties and/or fabric liner on the crotch of pants), or while sitting down, hold the back of the jeans at the top to make sure the placement of the jeans stays over the butt. This allows people to see the outfit and how great you look in it, rather than your butt and polka dot panties. Keep it classy and presentable.

HINT: Get your pants professionally hemmed. Many products temporarily "hem" pants with magnets or fabric tape.

Tops

Similar to jeans, tops are made in different styles, cuts, colors, and fits. Visit different stores to try on tops by color, cut, and size. When people compliment your body, listen to them and accentuate your asset with tops as well as with other clothing items. For example, if you get compliments on your eye color and your eyes are green, wear green tops; it will bring out the color of your eyes. If they complement you on your lovely long neck, show off that neck with V-neck tops.

If you work out and are proud of your back, purchase halter-tops and other low- or no-back tops. Keep in mind that proper undergarments must be worn at all times. Looking your best and feeling your best start with being presentable.

HINT: When buying tops try on several colors and related shades. Our skin tone can look dull or have a vibrant glow depending on the fabric and color.

Dresses and Skirts

Casual dresses and skirts come in all lengths. Daytime wear that is more than three inches above the knees should rarely be worn.

Maneuvering around the office, walking from class to class, or simply sitting at a coffee shop is complicated if you have to position yourself and pull down your skirt or dress every minute. Save the mini for events where you can look like a class act instead of a clueless one. Know which dresses and skirts you feel comfortable in as well as which look good on you. A gown or a street-length dress is made for evening events or black-tie weddings. A tea-length dress (see picture above) or a skirt is worn for daytime functions, and a cocktail dress can be worn for an evening or day event as long as your invite does not say black tie or floor-length dress. When an invitation requests a floor-length or black-tie dress, follow the request.

The three dress lengths are as follows…

Cocktail Dress

Length of dress/skirt above the knee.

Midi or Tea Length

Dress falls between the knees and the ankles.

Gown/ Maxi Dress

Dress hem must touch the floor or fall an inch above the floor. A gown can come as a two-piece set; therefore, the skirt must touch the floor. A maxi dress is the casual daytime version of the gown.

HINT: Not sure if your dress or skirt is too short for daytime wear? Pull a chair in front of your full-length mirror and sit down, and then stand up. If you cannot do so without adjusting your clothes to hide your undergarments, don't wear it.

"Drop" an item in front of your mirror and pick it up while looking at

yourself on the front and the back. If your private area has the chance of being made public, do not wear that dress or skirt.

Day-to-Day Clothing

We all know personal appearance matters not only when we go to work or school and parties. We also go to the gym, the supermarket, museums, etc. Dress for the occasion. If you're going to the gym, wear gym clothes. Don't put on oversized shirts and sweatpants with holes, as though you are cleaning the attic. Wear clothes that flatter your figure, but they should not be too revealing. Make sure the material absorbs sweat. If you are going to the market or bringing your dog to the groomer, never leave your house with rollers in your hair or a scarf tied around your head. Never step out in house shoes and pajamas. Never leave the house knowing that if the man of your dreams or your boss saw you, you would hide because you are dressed as though you just rolled out of bed instead of being dolled up as the gorgeous lady that you are. Lastly, if you are going to spend most of your day walking around museums and taking public transportations, wear comfortable shoes and clothes. You can always pack high heels in your bag to change into.

Dress to Impress

Many of us get dressed for work, take our time to apply makeup, run around in heels all day, and smile and entertain people until we are back home.

As soon as we walk through the door, we kick off our heels, wipe the day away, and slip on some pajamas or loungewear. If, when you get home, you only have to make dinner and then go straight to bed, by all means, slide into those comfy house shoes and pajamas; but if you are home early and would chat on the phone, run errands, invite friends over for a meal, or read a book in your favorite chair, then freshen up rather than drag around the house. Why give your best self to the world instead of enjoying your best self or sharing it with your family? You and your family deserve the best of you too. An easy way to break this habit is to invest in stylish casual or loungewear. Leave the pajamas in the bedroom, and use them only for bed. You don't have to look like a *Dynasty* character, but you want to relax in clothes that make you feel sexy and comfortable. Avoid stained shirts and sweatpants. These items are used as children's after-school play clothes. Change out of your work clothes and put on casual comfy pants or shorts and a clean top. Your significant other will notice your style, and your children will follow suit.

Undergarments

A great appearance doesn't start and end with the clothes and the shoes. Packaging yourself starts with wearing perfect panties, a properly fit bra, or any other undergarment.

Many stores have personnel who can take your measurements and find the bra that best fits you. Get those measurements and remember them. You should also take your bust, waist, and hip measurements. Write them down, and save them in your cell phone, in your laptop, or in your handy journal. Every woman should know her measurements.

HINT: Knowing your measurements not only helps you order clothes online but also makes it easy for a male friend or your husband to purchase clothes for you. It also helps a salesperson put your sizes aside for your future shopping trips and VIP treatment.

Bra

Bras come in different styles. Have at least one of each style that flatters your figure and gives you the support you need. Aside from having bras of different styles, which are listed below, invest also in nipple covers, bra padding, and a garment tape that enhances your cleavage and assists in coverage.

Bra Types: V-neck, Plunging, Push-up, Sports bra, Backless, T-shirt

Panties

They should always be worn for comfort *and* functionality. Fitted clothes normally call for a thong or a T-back, which avoids visible panty lines (VPL). Full back panties should be worn with full skirts or pants with pockets. Many women reserve several panties for their menstruation. Invest in cotton and silk panties and replace as needed. Accidental "leaks" during menstruation is common. Invest in dark-colored cotton panties so washing will be easy and you avoid trashing stained undies.

Shapers

Many companies make body shapers to smooth the extra rolls and shape our curves. Whether we are thin or plus size, shapers can give a helping hand to make us look great in everything we wear. Shapers are a wise investment for everyone and come in a range of styles for all different budgets.

Comfortable Wear for Clothing

Products today cater to everyday problems in an effort to make us look our best. Invest in products such as an underarm guard (it sticks to clothing underarms if you are prone to sweating), a double-sided tape to keep low-cut clothes in place or quickly hem pants, and nipple covers to conceal nipples when they are erect or when you go braless. These items will allow you to look your best without any worries.

Underwear, bras, pasties for nipple coverage, garment tapes, body shapers, etc., should never be visible in public. These items are called undergarments and intimates for a reason, so they are personal items for your eyes only. You should own several types of undergarments to address the different needs of all your clothes. The goal is to look effortlessly stylish. If your breasts are sagging or you're continuously tugging at your panties, you will look bad.

Many dresses and tops are designed to show your bra or your panties. These fashion styles are tricky and should only be worn as a fashion statement at appropriate events. When you do wear them, make sure you look great, feel good, and walk with confidence. When done right, they will make people think how they missed the fashion boat.

Undergarment Tips and Tricks

Sometimes I want my breast to have more cleavage or I want a panty-less look. I know we have to work with what God gave us, but here are a few tips to achieve the look.

You Want Larger Breasts or More Cleavage

Since doing pageants and working as a model I have learned several ways to make my B cups look like C's or D's.

1. Wear padded bras or insert breast enhancers into your bra. The true trick is pulling your breast skin (or fat) toward the top or front of your bra. The natural movement of your breast makes your enhancements look real.

2. An old fashion pageant trick is using tape: Bend over at the hips, take your breast and squeeze them together and lift. Take heavy duty tape and place one end of the tape on the lower outside area of one breast. Pull the tape under both breast and tape the other breast on the outside.

When you stand up straight your breast will appear fuller. You can also place enhancement cups between your breast and the tape. Use oil to remove the tape.

3. Sew or tape enhancement cups into your dress or top. This technique gives shape to the clothing and is great for backless items.

4. You can also purchase a "bra" that have adhesive that simply sticks to your skin.

Go Commando...AKA no undies

Some outfits call for nude colored panties or no panties at all. I always prefer to wear a G-string or flesh colored panties if I can. But I have worked on sets which wardrobe did not allow panty lines. You can choose to go commando, and wear nothing. But if you feel more comfortable with underwear this is my trick…

1. I purchase flesh colored thong or G-string undies. I cut the sides to remove the side band holding the front and the back in place.

2. I take double sided tape and line the top of the panties in the front and back.

3. Press and smooth the panties against your skin.

Dress Silhouettes

Dresses come in different shapes and styles. A dress silhouette is often discussed when a wedding dress or a bridesmaid dress is considered, but in our everyday lives, we will need a dress for special occasions. Knowing your body type will help you pick a dress silhouette that accentuates your body. Below are classic silhouettes and the body types they accentuate. Keep in mind that A-Line, Empire, and sheath can be of any length. The ball gown and trumpet normally kiss the floor.

Column/Sheath

A classic silhouette that is not tailored to fit your waist and curves. A sheath dress can be designed to be very dramatic and flatter the body by adding curve to the bust.

Mermaid/Trumpet

A fitted body conscious dress that is fitted from the bust to the knee area. The lower section of the dress has a full skirt. Hourglass figures and straight (ruler shape) bodies look best in a trumpet dress because it emphasizes and adds curves.

Empire (pronounced om-peer)

A high-waist dress that is gathered under the bust. The dress style can fit the waist or fall loosely below the bust. This classic fit can hide your unflattering parts while showing off your great assets. It makes bust look larger, petite women look taller. An empire also frames the face nicely, to show off your skin and neck.

A-Line

This dress has a silhouette of a capital "A." Most A-line dresses hug the waist, has fuller skirt, and a fitted bodice. The A-line compliments most body types.

Ball Gown

This Cinderella- like dress gives the illusion of a small waist since the dress has a very full skirt. Women with a pear shape or feel heavier on the lower half look fabulous in this style.

Special Occasions

Special occasions are normally a big event you will remember. Pictures are taken, you see old friends, and making new ones is possible. Pay close attention to what look you want to have, *not* just the outfit.

Packaging yourself well includes hair, nails, shoes, accessories, and makeup. No one looks great in a beautiful tailored dress and dirty nails, chipped polish, or oily hair. Look through fashion magazines and learn how you can recreate a fashionable style from head to toe. You can ask a salesperson at your favorite store, a department store fashion stylist, or a fashionable friend to help you plan your look. You may even consider having an image consultant. Remember, this night is about having a great time. You don't want to feel uncomfortable or worry about a falling up-do and a fashion malfunction.

HINT: Many boutiques and department stores offer a stylist's assistance for free or at a low cost. Call ahead of time to schedule an appointment.

Weddings, parties, theaters, and dates always seem to sneak up on us when we don't have a thing to wear. If we follow a few simple rules, we can always look great and feel great and have a memorable time.

Weddings and wedding-related events

Never wear white. Leave white to the bride. If you choose to wear a dress or a skirt, it should hit the knees no more than one inch above the knees. A cocktail dress can be worn to a rehearsal dinner and/or an engagement party.

Parties

Whether you are attending a dinner party or a house party, if you can, ask the host what the attire is. You don't want to arrive in jeans only to see everyone else in cocktail attire. If the host says, "Wear whatever you want, no dress code," ask what she is wearing, and then mirror her casual or dressy attire.

HINT: If you are not sure what the dress code is, always wear a little black dress or slacks with a nice blouse.

Dates

Ask your date what the attire is for the place you are going to. Wear clothes that complement your figure and leave something to the imagination. Your date will wonder what is underneath those clothes.

Let his mind wonder. Revealing clothes often come across as "trying too hard." You want to wear an outfit that shows your date you have good taste in clothes and you respect yourself. Always bring a purse large enough to fit a lipstick, a compact, and enough money to get you home in case your date turns sour.

After the first date and on the right date—like in a night club, at a private dinner party for two, or if you just want to look sexy for your date—wear the sexy outfit, or show some skin. Dressing more conservatively on the first date is not about hiding who you are. Wearing modest clothes allows your date to imagine you without clothes on. It also helps your date focus on what you're saying rather than on what you are wearing so you can get to know each other. When you pick an outfit that looks fabulous on you, your date is going to wonder what wonderful things he has to do for you to see the body that complements the clothes.

Personal Grooming

Create good personal grooming habits. Personal grooming depends on the individual. Grooming and maintenance should be private. Your body's up keep should never be noticed by the public, done in front of anyone, or seen as a lack thereof by anyone.

Dental Hygiene

Fresh breath is a must. Brush at least twice a day, and floss every day or as directed by your dentist. Your handbag should always have breath fresheners. Avoid gum. It's hard to talk to a person who is chomping on gum. Dental appointments and health care can be costly, but good dental hygiene can help maintain a healthy body and lifestyle. Yellow, chipped and crooked, and missing teeth can and will be looked at as low personal standards.

You should have high personal standards for yourself and a plan for maintaining a healthy body. Many dental offices help arrange a payment plan so you can look your best without blowing your budget. A beautiful and healthy smile is one of the first qualities a person notices in you and makes him or her see how you take care of yourself.

HINT: White teeth are a sign of good oral health. Teeth whitening products are sold at your local dentist's office, at the drugstores, and in high-end department stores at varying prices. I have used Opalescence Night White and Brite White products in the past. Currently, I whiten my teeth the old-fashioned way. I mix hydrogen peroxide and baking powder into a dry paste. I brush with the peroxide–baking powder mix once a day, and use regular toothpaste all other times.

Hair

Keep hair clean, trimmed, and healthy. Hairstyles are a personal choice that reflects your style. Have fun with your hair. Color it, braid it, wear an Afro, or blow it out straight to top off any look. Clean hair with trimmed ends is a must. Invest in a quality haircut. A great haircut will cut down your grooming time and create a flawless look every day. Ask your stylist for sample sizes of the products used on your hair. Take them home and see if you can maintain that salon look longer.

HINT: Clip-in extensions are a great way to create a new look. You can attach any type of weft hair to a toupee clip/comb. Clip-ins are used by many models and actresses to create longer, fuller, or highlighted hair, without committing to a complete change.

Nails

Your hands and feet are noticed, whether somebody tells you or not. Spending money on manicure and pedicure every week or every month is not feasible for many of us. Have your own manicure and pedicure kit at home and do your nails yourself. You can also invest in instant manicured nails that you can glue to your nails. Many instant nails look real and are of high quality. Instant "press on" nails are a perfect choice for a quick fix or a color change.

DIY Manicure & Pedicure
1. Clean nails with a nailbrush.
2. Soak your hands and feet in warm water. I put a drop of the body oil that I use in my bath.
3. Trim your nails to desired length and push back cuticles with an orange stick.
4. Dry and file your nails to desired shape and length.
5. Polish (one layer of base layer, two layers of color, one layer of top coat).
6. Wear hand and feet moisturizing gloves at night or when you are lounging around the house at least once a week.

If you are short on time, use this quick trick: After taking a shower or a bath, rub baby oil on your cuticles and push cuticles back with an orange stick or with your fingertips. Wipe down oil with nail polish remover to remove excess oil. Polish your nails with a pale-pink or pink-tinted clear nail polish once a week. This process fends off chips and hangnails, keeps nails shiny (even if you accidentally polished your cuticles), and keeps your hands and feet smooth because of the oil.

Makeup
Before makeup is applied, your skin should be the best it can be: clean, moisturized, and healthy. Makeup is supposed to accentuate the positive, not hide the negative. Most health care plans include dermatological care. Visit a dermatologist to treat the imperfections on your skin. For regular care, clean and moisturize your skin daily.

Makeup should be worn to complement your features. "Barely there" makeup is great for an everyday look. Heavier makeup can be worn for evening events. Like fashion, makeup trends change every season. Go to your local stores and test products. Allow the salesperson to show you their latest products. Take home samples and practice applying at home before you buy items. Taking home store samples before you buy a product allows you to monitor your use. If you don't use a makeup sample within one or two weeks, don't buy it. If you only need an item for one event, use the sample, and save your money for items you use regularly.

HINT: Before purchasing a new makeup product, I apply the product in the store and then walk around with the product on for the rest of the day.

If it still looks great after a few hours out, I return to the store and purchase the item. This tactic helps me avoid having the dreaded buyer's remorse and buying multiple makeup gimmicks I don't need.

Body

Your body should be clean and smell good at all times. If you are wearing a designer dress that smells like a used football uniform, no one will want to come near you and get to know you. Cleanliness is mandatory. Clean your body every day. If you are prone to sweating, buy travel-size body sprays and a deodorant and keep them in your car or in your purse so you can always freshen up. You can also purchase underarm moisture pads. You can buy them in fabric stores or department stores. You might also be more prone to sweating because of what you are wearing. Wear breathable fabrics, like cotton and silk. Avoid wearing polyester and other synthetic fibers for extended periods; these materials lock in body heat, causing you to sweat.

Hairy Subject

Female body hair removal is a personal choice, but poor maintenance is gross. Facial hair, chest hair, and leg and arm hair are common and may grow thicker, longer, or curlier—this varies from woman to woman. A *Fly girl* who practices personal care removes all visible body hair. Not removing or trimming underarm, pubic, chest, and facial hairs is considered poor hygiene.

Nips and Chest

If you grow hair around your nipples or on your chest, always pluck. Shaving and using depilatories may cause ingrown hairs.

Pubic Places

If you don't want to remove your pubic hair, trim it. You can have fun with it too. Many spa services and products allow you to shape, dye, and add crystals around your private area. You can make red hearts, a purple landing strip, or sparkling shapes. Here are some fun ideas for private parts grooming.

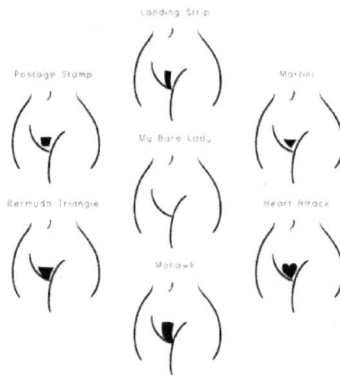

Cleanliness

Taking care of your personal appearance begins with how you keep your life in order. A clean and organized home help you keep a clean and organized appearance. If your clothes are on the floor, it is hard to keep them clean and wrinkle free. It becomes hard to distinguish clean clothes from dirty clothes when your room or your house looks as though a tornado whipped through it. Keep your living quarters clean and organized. Not only is it hard to welcome guests to a filthy home, it is also unhealthy to live in chaos.

HINT: When your items are strewn across the house or room, you spend more money on items you do not need as items are lost or damaged because of lack of care.

Keep your house and room clean and organized. Your personal life of filth and mess always spills over into the world around you. All notices the standards by which you carry yourself and deal with the world around you. If your life standards are low, people will treat you with the same low standards. Even if your man is dirty, he still doesn't want a dirty woman in his life. A healthy appearance inside out presents the best you so you can welcome new and old friends into your life and your home.

2

"Nothing makes a woman more beautiful than the belief that she is beautiful." – Sophia Loren

Be The Best You

I love to go out and get together with friends and meet new people. I read the newspaper frequently and watch the news. I also read literature and try to stay abreast of cultural and current events.

Well, this particular evening, I was not having much luck conversing with the people around me. My social awareness and knowledge of current events were falling short in the evening's robust conversations. My peers were dropping historical names, and they knew their facts. I ended up becoming the silent pretty girl in the room. I was ill prepared to interject my views on political events and give my opinions on the day's events.

In the end, I decided to leave early since I could not live up to my standards and take part in the conversations in an intelligent manner. I vowed to never let that happen again. Who wants to be Fly and dumb? Not me… and not you.

From that time on, I have made sure I am at my best inside and out. When I leave the house, I make sure I'm physically prepared for the day: I am wearing appropriate clothes and have read the morning paper.

Don't be the Fly girl with designer on the behind and nothing on the mind. My dad would say that to me and my three sisters.

HINT: *Purchase makeup remover wipes. Most women want to remove makeup once they arrive home and tie up their hair.*

Wipe your face clean of makeup, but keep your eye makeup on. Leaving on eye makeup makes you look "together," plus you have less to wash away at the end of the day.

Communication

Surprisingly, many of us speak with more respect and care to people outside the house than we do to the dearest people in our homes. We unconsciously take for granted the love of our family and closest friends because we know they will always love us unconditionally; people outside the home, on the other hand, may choose to associate with us or not. Don't treat your family and friends this way. Bad behavior will only alienate and cause resentment within the home, making home life increasingly troublesome. Always talk to your loved ones as though it is your last day on earth. It may be hard when you are in conflict with them, but your efforts could ease a more serious tension.

Talk to Yourself with Love

Many times, we talk to ourselves worse than anyone else does. When we gain a few pounds, we call ourselves fat. When we do not achieve our goal, we tell ourselves, "I'm terrible at this. Why do I keep trying?"

Be kind to yourself. We all have shortcomings and become angry when we fail at something, but allow the better part of you to accept your shortcomings and find a way to change and improve. If you say kind words to yourself, people will respect you more because you will demand from them the kind of respect you give yourself.

Build your Communication Skills Inside Out

You should read more to build your vocabulary and enhance your communication skills. Reading improves your vocabulary, allows you to be well versed in many subjects, and makes you a more interesting person because you have more sources to draw from in forming an opinion. People have a higher respect for knowledgeable people who speak with substance than for those who just voice their opinions based on their emotions.

Ten Books Every Woman Should Read

How to Win Friends and Influence People, by Dale Carnegie

To Kill a Mockingbird, by Harper Lee

Lolita, by Vladimir Nabokov

The Bell Jar, by Sylvia Plath

I Know Why the Caged Bird Sings, by Maya Angelou

The Bible, Quran, or Tanakh

Women & Money, by Suze Orman

The Five Love Languages, by Gary Chapman

The Beauty Detox Solution, by Kimberly Snyder, C.N.

Pride and Prejudice, by Jane Austen

Add-Ons

7 Habits of Highly Effective People, by Stephen R. Covey

Why Men Love Bitches, Sherry Argov

As I stated previously, you should also read the paper or the online news every day. Take time to watch news broadcast to stay abreast of the day's events and current affairs. Your knowledge on life and the world around you and your personal understanding of yourself will allow you to communicate with other people with ease.

We also have the opportunity to become more knowledgeable using the latest technology. Download applications that allow you to read materials on current events, learn a new word every day, and stay abreast of political affairs while standing in line for your daily coffee fix.

Must-Have Apps for Knowledge

Vocabulary

White House

News

Beauty Tips

The above applications and other similar ones can be added to your mobile phone for convenient access. Download applications for your local paper or your favorite news program. We all have a few minutes every day at random times where we pull out our phones and learn something rather than engage in idle chitchat.

HINT: Use the worksheet in the back of this book to clearly identify your interests, likes and dislikes, and knowledge of the world. If you know yourself well, you can express your views more clearly. As Maya Angelou says, "When you know better, you do better."

Arguments and Conflicts

If a problem arises, approach the concerned person directly rather than spreading news around to family and friends, hoping it gets to the person you are displeased with. This behavior is passive and puts you in a powerless position. You are stronger than that. So don't involve outsiders. It is easy for family and friends to get involved in a conflict with people they love and take sides. Going to the concerned person to air out your grievances will prevent the molehill from turning into a mountain with everyone involved.

Public Displays of Drama

You should never argue and yell at your significant other in front of anyone. Always pull the person aside to address an issue. If the conflict takes place in public, wait until you are behind closed doors and the two of you are alone. If it arises in front of your children, close friends, or family, wait until you two are alone and ready to talk, then discuss the problem.

An onlooker might relay what he or she saw and heard and use the conflict to drive a wedge between you and the person you love. Tempers flare and conflicts are common, but how you handle a conflict will be remembered and carried over into everyday life. Children will also imitate your behavior and language, even if you tell them otherwise and teach them good manners. People will see the way you treat your loved ones, and they will mimic your behavior and will soon treat your loved ones the way you treat them. Show respect for yourself and the people around you, and the world will follow.

Table Manners

When sitting at a table, both feet should be planted on the ground. Your back should be straight and slightly touching the back of the chair. Sitting with your back against the back of the chair helps you avoid slouching your shoulders forward. When you sit up straight, you look confident and more engaged with the people around you. Your distance from the table should be enough for you to move your arms and hands freely from your lap to the table and the plate. Sitting too far from the table and food will almost guarantee your food will fall on your clothes. Sit at the table comfortably so you can bring the food to your mouth and reach for your napkin with ease.

Manners are the same, whether you are having a dinner party, eating at a fancy restaurant, or sitting at a table with your family. Sexual, bathroom, or private conversations should not be engaged in at the dinner table.

Schedule a convenient time for the family to sit down for dinner as often as possible. In today's world, families are busy with sports, work, social clubs, etc.; and a family dinner is important to keep each family member abreast of each other's life. Schedule a supper with your family at least once or twice a week if every day is impossible. Sundays are perfect days for bonding.

If you are single and do not have a family, schedule a weekly supper with your friends or your roommate. It will be a special and relaxing time for you and your friends to bond. Dinners with loved ones will force you to avoid taking phone calls and watching television during meals. Devoting a portion of your day or your week to the people you choose to share a meal and conversation with gives you something to look forward to and stops you from doing errands and tasks during the time that you are supposed to focus on yourself and your relationships.

Remove books, newspapers, magazines, laptops, readers, etc., from the table. Germs are everywhere, and these items are distractions. Think how many people have touched those papers, books, and magazines, and you can imagine the amount of germs in those materials, and you do not want those microbes near your food. Electronic devices should also be kept away from your food and off the table because we rarely clean them.

3

"T.H.I.N.K.- Is it True, Helpful, Inspiring, Necessary, and Kind?" – Unknown

Well Said...

Introducing oneself is one of the hardest things to do for some people, a walk in the park for others. On many occasions, such difficulty depends on whom you are introducing yourself to, how many people are listening and watching, what the event is, or whether you are familiar with anyone in the room. Although introducing yourself is simply saying your name, one thing rings true: People form an opinion about you before you open your mouth and as you say your first words.

Sometimes that opinion follows you throughout your life, and other times you get the opportunity to know a person more, beyond your first meeting. With luck and care, a long friendship can be formed.

Introductions

When introducing yourself, hold out your right hand and reach for the other person's hand. Give a firm handshake, as if you are lifting a glass of water. Look the other person in the eye and smile. Do not look down at his or her hands or at anything else. Wandering eyes can be seen as lack of interest, and looking down may be taken as insecurity or looking at the breasts or the body of the other person. The palm of your hand should touch the other person's palm, and your fingers should wrap under his or her hand. Don't squeeze or shake too hard. Allow the hands to naturally part. Do not give a soft handshake; it feels like a dead fish in the other person's hand. No one likes a limp handshake.

If you suffer from mysophobia (germaphobe), note that a person whom you meet for the first time does not know that. If he or she extends his or her hand, meet it with a handshake. It is rude and unwelcoming to leave a potential friend's hand hanging in the air. To avoid the awkward situation and the handshake, smile and look the person in the eye, clasp your hands together up to your chest or straight down in front of you, and then lean slightly forward and introduce yourself. The person will not reach for your hand to shake if your hands are clasped together, but your excitement to meet him or her will show in your voice and your eyes.

Remember, it is always best to shake a person's hand, but people today are more understanding of phobias. You don't have to let everyone know your phobias, and with tact and grace, you will be remembered as the lovely person with a great smile rather than the girl with the phobia.

As you and the other person are shaking hands, you give your name and he or she gives his or hers. Say your full name clearly and explain why you are attending the event or what your relationship to the host is.

Example: "Hello, I'm Jane Smith. Suzie and I went to college together."

Such introduction allows a person to throw follow-up questions and know you better or find a possible connection between you and him or her besides being at the same event or having a common friend.

HINT: If a person does not explain why he or she is at the event or how he or she knows the host, just ask.

Example: "How do you know Suzie?"

Such question will help you and the other person find a common ground for you two to get to know each other, even if he or she is shy.

Once the person has said his or her name, you must try very hard to remember it. One trick is to repeat the name at the end of your conversation. People naturally like to hear their names.

Example: "John, it was great meeting you. Have fun on the fishing trip."

"Robert, I'm so happy to hear you will be joining our study group."

This technique allows the brain to match the name with the face and register a connection to everyday life.

HINT: The best introductions are clear and direct. Many people are very shy or have speech impediments. If you have difficulty introducing yourself, inhale a slow full breath of air. Then say your name slowly with a smile as the air exits your lungs.

Do not hold your breath. Practice this a few times before you leave the house or while you are in the car with a friend, if you are going with a friend. Your mouth (lips, tongue, jaw, etc.) will get used to the pattern of movement, making it easier for you to control your nerves and do the introduction.

Introducing Other People

The proper way to introduce people is by rank, age, or sex. A man is introduced to a woman, a lower-titled person is introduced to a higher-titled person, and young people are introduced to old people. Give people their full names (titles if necessary) and what they may have in common.

HINT: Imagine introduction as a circle of friends or a group. You present the person to the circle. This allows the receiver of the introduction to welcome the person with comfort since you are introducing them.

Example: "Jane Smith, I would like to introduce you to John Brown. John, this is Jane. She is traveling to Italy in a few months. John has been to

Italy several times."

"Mr. Jones, I would like to introduce you to my good friend Bob Grey. Bob, John is my supervisor. Bob is starting a company on the second floor of our building."

Making an Exit

The most awkward part of meeting a person and making introductions is stepping away from a bad conversation or making sure you mingle with other guests. The exit is always tough, but it can be done respectfully and graciously. Exiting a conversation should leave open the opportunity for you and the other person to talk or meet again and make him or her feel good meeting you.

If you are the host of the party, the guests know and understand that you must mingle with everyone. So you can always excuse yourself politely and inform the person you are talking to how lovely it has been meeting him or her, thank him or her for coming, and explain that you must tend to other guests.

Example: "Jane, I am so happy you could make it. Please excuse me. I'm going to check on the roast."
"John, thank you for the wine. I'm going to put it aside right now."

Making a clean break from a casual conversation can be done perfectly. Excuse yourself without making a person feel unimportant or being rude. Give a closing statement, and then exit.

Example: "Suzie, it was a pleasure meeting you. Please excuse me."
If the person you are conversing with is someone you would like to have further contact with, ask him or her for his or her business card and/or offer grabbing coffee or drinks with him or her some other time. This allows you to get to know other people at the event and stay in touch with the people you have a special interest in. Offering your card first puts the person on the spot, so don't offer unless he or she asks. Always bring business cards. Don't pull out your phone and enter the other person's phone number, unless

you are a teenager and do not need business cards, or you know him or her well and you are in a place where only you can hear the number. It is unsafe and careless for him or her to announce his or her phone number. This rule applies to exchanging e-mail addresses in public as well.

Great Conversations

Between your wonderful entrance and your grand exit, you will get into many conversations.

Entering a conversation and keeping it going may seem daunting, but once you become comfortable with the give-and-take, it will be a breeze and far less agonizing even with the most aggressive talker.

Before you arrive at a party, a date, or a casual meeting, read on current events. Don't rely on news on TV for information because many networks have turned to commentary shows rather than reporting. Commentary and biased news reports only give you another person's opinion instead of allowing you to form your own based on the facts provided. Make it your duty to inform yourself, form an opinion, and then watch the correspondents deconstruct the latest events. Reading local, national, and international news keeps you abreast of everything that is going on around you and allows you to start a new conversation topic when there is a lull. The most engaging people are those who are aware of the events around the world and can form independent opinions about them.

Blood, Sweat, and Tears

Read materials on wars, local crimes, politics, and religion; but don't bring up such topics in conversations. These are subjects that most people hold very dear to their hearts and have strong feelings and personal opinions about and could make a conversation turn very sad or very heated. Leave these issues to conversations with close friends and family because they will still love you whatever their reaction is, plus they will probably agree with some of your opinions because they are your friends. Spare your new listener the pain that such themes bring.

Talk about the art showing at the local mall or the new exhibit at the local museum. These subjects can always progress to politics.

Example: "The new wing of the museum is going to create more jobs for the local community. I'm excited about that. What do you think?"

This open-ended question and conversation starter allows the listener to respond without a *yes* or *no* answer, and it tells him or her that you are happy about new jobs and that your interests include museums.

If your conversation partner turns the chitchat into something negative and uncomfortable, politely inform him or her that you have never really considered his or her opinion, and then shift the subject to how much you like the host and the party. Then begin your exit. We all run into the gloom-and-doom guest at parties. When you start your conversation with how you know the host or why you are attending the event, you allow an easy conversation to start and find interest in branching off the main topic.

Example: Jane: "Nice to meet you. I'm Jane Smith. I was Suzie's roommate in college. How do you know Suzie?"

Bob: "I met Suzie while working at the local bookstore down the street from college."

Jane: "Wow, I loved going to that bookstore. It had all our textbooks for us to rent. Suzie and I always got our books and coffee there."

Keep conversations light and find a common ground. Find something to compliment the person on. Everyone loves a compliment on an outfit choice. Let him or her know he or she looks great. You'll make his or her day, and night. Starting a conversation with a compliment eases the tension and helps gear the conversation in a direction where you and the person can find what you have in common. You'll leave the night making a new friend. When you compliment the person, do not ask about or give prices, sale items, etc. The cost or value of an item should never enter the conversation.

Example: "I had to come over and compliment you on your outfit. I love the new fall look with full skirts and tailored suits."

If you are given a compliment, just say, "Thank you, I love it too," or, "Thank you, it's so comfortable." Do not explain away the compliment by informing the person that your outfit was on sale, you feel fat in it, it's so old, etc. Women tend to deflect compliments as if they don't deserve them. Say, "Thank you," and enjoy that someone thinks you look fabulous.

You don't want to turn down a compliment, and you don't want to gild the lily. Don't overindulge in the compliment unnecessarily.

Example: Jane: "Suzie, you look good in that sweater."

Suzie: "Thank you. I love the feel of this cashmere on my skin. It's luxury that makes me look so slim. Plus, John just got me these pearls that complement the entire outfit."

Overextending a compliment is self-indulgent. Avoid it. A simple thank-you goes a long way and is warm and welcoming to the person giving the compliment.

What you like and dislike is also a great conversation piece. Before you got to a party or an event, know what your interests are. Know yourself. If you just went to Hawaii and loved the surfing lesson you took, talk about it. If your favorite band is coming to town in a month, share your excitement about rock music and the band's upcoming concert. If you like an author's style, race cars, junk food, or everything about celebrity life, talk about it so people get to know what is dear to you. A current event or popular news can be related in some way to your interests. People like talking to interesting people. If you don't have interests or don't know how to articulate them, people will not be interested in talking to you.

Don't force your topic on people by stirring the conversation to your interests. Two or more people make a conversation of equal give-and-take. The discourse is not a stage for you to perform on or a soapbox for you to preach from, vent on, or ask people to love what you love. Share your interests; then ask about theirs.

Example: Bob: "The weather is going to be great this weekend. This gives me a chance to go mountain biking. Do you like biking?"

Jane: "No, but I've gone hiking a few times. What trails do you use to go mountain biking?"

This conversation is give-and-take for both Bob and Jane. They shared their interests, allowing each one of them to elaborate on their hobbies. This conversation would naturally move to trails and mountains, which interest both Bob and Jane.

If the conversation doesn't continue on to your interests, do not redirect it to mountain biking or hiking. You only torture the person and ultimately push him or her away. If you are talking to someone who wants to push his or her agenda, start making your exit statement as soon as he or she completes his or her statement. Then exit with grace.

Progressive Conversation Topics
Hobbies
News (light topics)
Movies
Books
Work
Fashion
Sports
Weather
Events

Conversation Pitfalls
In today's world of reality shows and TV and online dating, we often see conversations take a wrong turn. Bad conversations make everyone within earshot, including the talker sometimes, feel uncomfortable. Many people make a conversation turn wrong because of nerves; others purposely

do it to get attention. You should avoid bad conversations no matter what.

We discussed previously conversation topics that are bad—wars, local crimes, politics, and religion. Anything you shouldn't and wouldn't do in public should not be discussed in public. That means no sex talk.

Sex is private and personal; keep it that way. You might end up talking to a person you are physically attracted to, and he or she begins a conversation about sex. Change the subject to get her or him back to a more comfortable and appropriate subject so he or she will get to know you and your interests outside the bedroom. If he or she goes back to a sexually charged talk, begin your exit statement. You may be attracted to her or him, but he or she is not interested in what you do outside the bedroom. You may be entangled in a conversation with someone who enjoys talking about anything that takes place in the bathroom. Again, change the subject, and then exit.

Sex, sexuality, and bathroom talks are tacky conversations. They also show that you have a limited knowledge of the world around you, as well as limited social interests. If you are the type of person who feels comfortable discussing your private life with the world, work hard to stop this habit. Read books, learn quotes, and talk about your quirky interests so people will have a chance to get to know you outside the bedroom and the bathroom. If you cannot engage your grandparents in such dirty talks, don't bother pulling anyone else in.

Conversation Topics to Avoid
War
Murder (crimes)
Sex
Bathroom Habits
Religion
Political Parties
Being Dumped
Drugs
Illness or Death
Gossip

The above topics can make anyone look bad and detract people from considering you as good company. Respect yourself and give your best to the people around you. Allow them to get to know you, and give yourself a chance to get to know them.

Make a Fierce Entrance and a Grand Exit

Making an entrance is very crucial as people form an impression of you. It also shows the world what you think of the host and how you carry yourself as a lady. Always be on time. If you are going to be late, let the host know before the event.

In the age of technology—where there are cell phones, e-mail, etc.—there is no excuse to not informing the host of your tardiness. We also have the Internet and GPS, so the host does not have to constantly answer your phone calls as you explain how lost you are or how extremely late you are going to be. Problems arise, and people do get lost and often get stuck in traffic; a gracious host understands when we get into such situations. If you are always late, however, people will notice it and stop inviting you to events, especially to those that are time-sensitive. Be respectful of people's time. Once you RSVP, make it a point for you to use the Internet to search for directions and set a reasonable amount of time for travel. If you came late to an event, don't make it the subject of the entire night. Apologize and move on to other topics in your conversations.

Making an entrance also involves bringing a gift. Wine and candy are great gifts to the host of the party. These are items that the host may use during the party or save for later. If you want to give flowers, send them ahead of time or earlier in the day. The host shouldn't have to leave the party to tend to your gift (cutting flower stems and putting them in water). If you bring food, know the taste, allergies, and style of the host. You don't want to give treats that the receiver cannot enjoy.

HINT: If time allows, give a gift the host will enjoy personally. He or she will be impressed that you cared enough to find the right gift rather than doing it as an afterthought.

Fashionably Late

At small and quaint events, arrive on time or within five to ten minutes from start time. Do *not* arrive over twenty minutes late. That is a blatant disregard for the host and her guests. A person can be fashionably late to certain events. Normally, being fashionably late is reserved for the host, not for the guest at large events. It makes you look busy and important to most people. It also makes sure that you are not walking into an empty hall, waiting for people to arrive. For club parties, company parties, and very large events (excluding weddings and birthday parties), you may arrive five to thirty minutes after the start time. In some cases, you can arrive up to an hour late . . . and still be right on time. Your time of arrival depends on what or whom the party is for and what types of activities are being held.

Fashionably Late Guide

EVENT	FASHIONABLE
Dinner Party	0–10 minutes late
Small Gatherings	5–15 minutes late
Club Party	30–45 minutes late
Fashion Show	On time
Lunch, Brunch, Dinner Date	On time, never late
Keg Party	15–30 minutes late
Company Party	15–30 minutes late

Gauge your time of arrival based on the events that will take place. If a fashion show starts at 5:00 p.m., be at the event early enough to find your seat and settle and speak to fellow guests. If you are attending a birthday party at a large venue, arrive before any activities begin (presentation of hired performers, cake cutting, singing "Happy Birthday"). Arriving after or during these activities may be seen as narcissism and self-indulgence. Being gracious, humble, and caring is a much better trait, no matter how "important" or popular you are.

The Exit

Making a grand exit does two things: it leaves people wanting more of you and makes you never look desperate. Having one of the best nights of your life is no excuse for dancing on the dance floor while the cleaning crew tries to sweep around you or talking the host's ear off about the fabulous guy you met earlier. Don't close down the party. Know when to go home . . . or at least get the heck out of there. The host and the crew have to wait until everyone is gone to start the cleanup process. The longer you stay, the longer their night of cleaning is. Never stay at a nightclub until the lights turn on or the DJ announces last song, last call, or last anything. Lingering gives the impression that you are desperate and bored with your life.

A grand exit allows you to mingle and exit on your terms. If you stay in a conversation too long, or if you stay at a bar for too long, an onlooker will see you as someone who has nothing better to do in life. If you have nothing better to do than overextend your welcome at a friend's house or wait for the owner or the DJ to kick you out of the club, your life must be pretty boring.

No one wants to meet, get to know, or get involved with a person who has nothing better to do with himself or herself. Ask yourself; Do you like meeting boring people? Do you like hanging out with a friend who is desperate for anything? Everyone likes to be surrounded with confident, fun, interesting people. Be that confident, fun, interesting person you want to be. If you don't feel that way yet, fake it until you become it.

When making your grand exit, you must make sure all special activities have been done. Do not leave before the wedding cake is cut, "Happy Birthday" is sung, or the dessert is served, eaten, and cleared. Leaving before the main event is rude, unless you have an emergency to tend to. Always compliment fellow guests around you, thank them for their time, find the host and compliment her on her event, and then exit. You don't have to announce your exit to the entire party. The most important person is the host, not you.

Grand Exits

Conversation with a fellow guest
After ten minutes, excuse yourself. Do not ask for his or her card. Offer your card and suggest talking at later in the evening or some other time.

Leaving a small house party
Say good-bye to everyone. Compliment the host.

Club
Leave within three hours.

Birthday, engagement, dedication party
Don't be the last one standing around.

Dinner party
When the meal is finished, gauge the rest of the evening. If all activities

have been done, thank the host and bid farewell to the guests.

Lunch, dinner, brunch date
Within fifteen to thirty minutes after a dropped check. The waiter needs his table to make money and survive. The longer you stay, the less money he or she makes.

We all have experienced a great time, but leave people wanting for more. Allow them to miss you and wonder about your busy schedule. That is a grand exit.

If you are asked why you are leaving, don't lie or give excuses. Inform your fan(s) you have a busy day tomorrow. You need not bore them with details. Who cares if you're really going home to change your cat's litter box?

Under some circumstances (gathering with close friends), you have no reason to make a grand exit. Buddy up and walk each other to your cars, or help a friend clean up since she made you and your gal pals a wonderful dinner. By all means, hang out and finish that last bottle of wine you brought. Making a grand exit at your best friend's party is uncalled-for if you are just going to call your friends to complain about how bored you are.

Thank You
A grand exit is not complete without a handwritten thank-you card for the host. Within the first two days after the party, send a thank-you card for her or his hard work in organizing a great event as well as sharing an experience in his or her life with you. Do not send an e-mail. No one is that busy not to have time to send a card.

HINT: Always buy thank-you cards when you see them on sale, even if you have no use for them at the time of the purchase. If you have it, you will send them.

Thank-you notes are great for any occasion. If you met someone and had a pleasant conversation, a person would show you a pleasant gesture. Or if you want, you can send a quick thanks for a little gift a person gave you. A thank-you card from you will always be remembered and appreciated. It is best to send a thank-you within the first week, but if you forget, send it at any time, but ASAP. If you send a thank-you note late, admit your blunder and explain how you have been thinking about the person and that you really wanted to send the note.

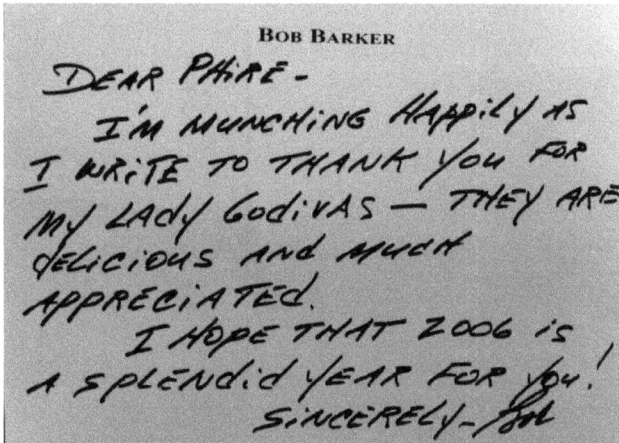

Bob Barker sent me a handwritten thank you card at eighty-four. If he can find the time and energy to write a thank you card and mail it, there is no reason you or I cannot send a thank you to a friend.

4

"You're never going to see me coming out of the club at two a.m. with my weave all hanging off, getting in somebody's car." –
Tyra Banks

Social Grace

The one question I am asked most after working on *The Price Is Right* is if my fellow models and I got along. I give a resounding *yes!* While working on the show, I became very close to the other ladies. We had wonderful social outings after work and during our off time. We shared our lives, talked about our dreams, and are currently good friends. In our gatherings, we all talk at once, jumping in and out of conversations and moving from one subject to the next with ease. This quality is our common ground and an understanding we share. We take turns talking and listening, never belittling or judging. Our friendships work because we respect each other.

All relationships are give-and-take, so give your best self and people will give the same. Be a listener. Share your heartfelt opinions. Give of yourself. If you feel your best is being taken advantage of, you must confront the situation or leave it as it is. Sometimes you realize that a social situation is just not right for you. Sometimes being the best you can be means walking away when someone else's best is not good enough for you. Recognize the signs (lying, taking your material goods, tardiness, belittling your goals and dreams, etc.). When you are friends with many people and your friendship is a unit, don't allow one person to degrade you. Large social outings can be harder to walk away from because many people are tied together. Stick up for yourself, address the problem person directly, and move on. Don't wait for other people in your group to fight for you. Avoiding the problem or waiting for another person to fix the conflict for you will only put you in a weak position, and you will always need another person's assistance to help you out of a conflict.

Groupies

One of the most common social events today is hanging out in groups rather than having one-on-one dates. Group outings are great because there is safety in numbers and the likelihood of meeting like-minded people and finding common characteristics, goals, and hobbies is great and rare. Group outings, however, can be a challenge because of multiple personalities. Going to such outings means you must be compromising, open-minded, selfless, and willing to share. Although a group might look like a laundry list of characteristics, fitting in is easy when you have something in common, whether it's school, a hobby, or work. With a few simple etiquette guidelines, you can have a pleasurable time with other people, and they will enjoy having you around.

Driving

If you are not the driver, respect the driver's space and practice safety. Do not eat and leave trash in the car. Do not change the radio station or adjust anything in the car without asking for permission. A car is like a person's home; everything in it caters to it owner's needs, not the passenger's. So sit back and do not block or distract the driver.

Distracting the driver with pictures, phone calls, food, etc., can make him or her take her or his eyes off the road to respond to you, which can lead to an accident. Avoid telling him or her how terrified you are of car accidents, other drivers, and driving. It is okay to express your concern for safety, but a constant reminder of your anxieties will not put the driver at ease to get you to your destination safely. If your anxiety is that extreme, insist on driving yourself and spare your friends the distress.

If you are the driver, keep your eyes on the road, do not drink, and avoid distractions from your passengers. Implement the "no phone zone" rule in your car. Install a Bluetooth connection and audio GPS to your car to avoid handling calls and pages of handheld directions. Your passengers will see that their safety is important to you and will respect you for it.

Dining

Rotate which friend you sit next to each outing. Get to know each person equally so you will understand everyone's personality. Rotating also helps avoid cliques within a group of friends. Table manners are just as important in a casual atmosphere with friends as they are in an extravagant event. If you behave differently on different occasions, others may see this inconsistency as a fake or a façade. Be true. Be your best at all times.

All diners should pay their share of the leisure dining. Agree beforehand whether the bill will be split evenly or each person will pay for his or her meal. If the contributions come short of the total bill, try to correct the shortage by working out the balance among the diners. If the problem cannot be solved, offer to chip in more money, if you can afford it. If this always happens, inform your friends you only brought enough cash for your share. If the problem persists, one friend may be the root of the problem. Pull that person aside and address your concern politely and discreetly.

The Clique

Everyone has her or his close group of friends, which may be seen as a clique by others. In grade school, many of us know the popular group and the not-so-popular group. A person who has worked to be good inside and out understands that no matter what ranking society places them in, they should give best full respect to everyone. An intern, a less popular coworker, or a service person is addressed with the same respect accorded to a superior or a friend.

Genetics, finances, social class, and being victims of circumstances and disability are often situations people are born into and have no control over. They often place people in or out of a group. Be mindful and encourage your group of friends to be mindful and empathize. A person who belittles the less fortunate is not a person of honor and is seen as someone who has inferior character and many hidden flaws. Set a standard for yourself regardless of how other people in the group behave. Define yourself and be the Fly girl with etiquette. Do not let your friends or acquaintances define you and shape your life with bad behavior.

Time Management

Always be on time for any engagement when meeting with a friend or a small group of friends. Being fashionably late is acceptable if you are attending an event that is on a large scale. A constantly late person or a no-show after he or she has confirmed her or his attendance is seen as selfish because of the importance he or she places only on her or his own life rather than on the disposition of other people. True friends do not behave this way. If you are not sure if you can attend a date or arrive on time, inform your group of friends, and they will understand. It is rude to keep anyone waiting for you.

Many adults live with curfews and rules. Accept those rules and respect them whether you believe in them or not. Respecting your friends' standards shows that you respect her or him and his or her beliefs.

Communication

Gossiping about anyone within your group of friends or outside your circle should be frowned upon. This habit creates negative energy, and the gossiper is looked upon as someone who is being adolescent and having low self-esteem. When problems between you and a friend arise, address the involved person directly. Avoid the fifth-grade mentality. Don't spread a story in your group or try to tarnish a person's reputation. You never end up looking good or in control by spreading stories. The result is you lose a friend and you look pretty ugly in front of your friends.

More Than Friends

Dating a friend is normal. Each person has a unique personality, and you and a friend may have a common ground that you bond together more than you do with the other people in your group. Keep your private life private. With luck and care, your relationship will blossom into something special and long lasting; but if that relationship ends, do not share the details of its demise. If your ex-partner decides to share the story of your escapades as well as criticize your behavior in public, do not take part in it. This type of a man is not the one you want to keep in your life. He is not a gentleman, nor is he a man who is worth your effort defending yourself. Share your pain and the details of your story with your family and closest confidants only. Don't make your relationship and its failure a public spectacle. It will only make you look as bad as or worse than your crumbled relationship, allowing every onlooker and listener to criticize you.

You Dropped Something . . .

It is just as important to not discuss finances and price tags with friends, as it is to not do it with a complete stranger. Don't drop (share) price tags, names, income, and brands. This habit shows low self-esteem and lack of values in meaningful conversations. Don't ask friends how much their items cost or share how much your wardrobe cost. It is wonderful to share your efforts and journey in asking for a raise but tasteless to share how much your paycheck is. It is equally important for you to never ask how much a friend earns. If he or she wants to share this information with you, she or he will share it without you having to pry.

Just as you don't share the names of your fashion brands to show your status, you don't drop names of people you know if they have nothing to do with the topic at hand. Do not share the names of your past and current love interests, no matter how famous these people are or how high their status.

Giving the names and the details of your "conquests" only makes you look like a status seeker and a fame whore, in the worst way. Inquiring minds may want to know, but dishing about your love life places you in a position where you sound as though you are trading your body for social status. Dating prominent men is fine and, in some cases, expected, but you should climb the social ladder on your own merits, not by riding on the coattails of the men you bed.

Keep Friends Close

Friendships go through cycles that are similar to the phases of life and romantic relationships. Expect changes brought on by careers, relocation, personal experiences, and interests. Moving from one cycle to the next does not mean the end of a friendship. Reach out to old and new friends during reasonable hours. Make phone call appointments and stick to the time so you can keep in touch, and stay abreast of the most interesting details in each other's life.

When you see old friends, ask them about their lives first before you spill your blood, sweat, and tears. Communication is a give-and-take; make sure you give of yourself just as much as you take from others.

HINT: When meeting with friends for shopping trips or a girls' night out, pack little treats your friends like. If you have a friend who loves to chew gum after a meal, carry an extra packet of her favorite gum in your purse. Find an eye shadow that your friend has been dying to try; buy it as an inexpensive "thanks for being a friend" token. Little treats go a long way.

Gossip

Don't spread news about a friend or a foe, whether it is true or false, juicy or dry. This is a personal rule you must have for yourself. Gossip has become so acceptable in today's society because of the multitude of gossip magazines, entertainment shows, and social networks that keep you up-to-date on the breaking news around town or, simply, among friends. Spreading gossip can be very tempting, but you can surely stop yourself from whispering the latest hot topic you heard about your neighbor by asking yourself, "If I spread this bit of gossip, what does this say about me?" Gossiping says a lot about you. Your gossiping habits tell a person that...

- You cannot be trusted with information
- Your life is pretty boring, so you want to talk about someone else's life
- You haven't read the paper in weeks
- You're so desperate to be liked by people that you'll spread stories about someone so that they'll talk to you.

When you hear someone gossip about other people, listen closely to the ticking of the clock, and eventually, that person will gossip about you to the rest of the world. It doesn't feel good knowing that he or she is going to spread stories about you to everyone you know and may not know instead of coming to you directly or not spreading gossip about you at all.

Keep in mind that a gossip has been known to ruin lives, and it is rarely correct. Don't give in to this bad habit. You want to be seen as a true friend, whether you and the person concerned are best friends or acquaintances. If you find that the town gossiper has perched herself or himself next to you, as he or she spills all the latest "he said, she said," change the subject.

Bring out the most popular gossip magazine article, or just ask how the gossiping person is doing. You can also politely excuse yourself from the conversation. That person will know you are not the type to gossip and will respect you for that. Putting your best foot forward starts with you.

Personal Questions

Many of us have asked questions that have made us want to scurry away or literally put our feet in our mouths to shut ourselves up. We normally ask a personal question that embarrasses another person and/or ourselves. It happens. Apologize and move forward. Having social grace will help you avoid embarrassing moments like these.

Don't ask the following questions

- Are you pregnant? How many months?
- Did you get work [plastic surgery] done?
- Is all "that" [weave, hair, eyelashes, nails] yours?
- How much do you weigh?
- How much was _____?
- Your natural color [skin or hair] is _____.

One way to determine whether you should or should not ask: if the question you are about to ask should be talked about with a doctor, lawyer, banker or finance professional, or beautician, don't ask.

If a person really wants to share information, you would already know. Don't be offended if the person doesn't want to talk about her true hair color, weight, latest Botox session, or pregnancy. Many people have their reasons for keeping parts of their lives private, even if these details are obvious to you and the rest of the world. You would never want to put yourself in a position where you would be told to "mind your own business."

Consideration + Honesty + Respect = Honor

Most of us are raised in today's world aware that our opinions count. We are important and special. We are trained to always say what we feel. We have freedom of expression. That is true, but enjoying this freedom does not mean making it less true for other people. Having consideration and humility is tough in a world where the rudest reality star gets his or her own show or helps a politician win his or her campaign.

You can move up the ranks in your company or become more popular by being self-indulgent, rude, and never considering how your actions will affect another person; but you will not have honor, respect, and/or dignity. Your importance does not make another person less important.

My mother often told me to never do anything that would make me hold my head down in shame or leave me wanting to avoid a person. Not considering another person's feelings when you do or say something can be seen as selfishness and egotism, which we know are bad traits. Our great self-esteem should not come at the expense of others. When you belittle a person or do not give your best self to everyone, it is noticed by all, whether you think somebody sees you or not. You want to be part in cheering up someone or understanding her or him.

By considering the feelings of the people around you who may be affected by your actions, you show personal grace and high regard for yourself and what you stand for. This trait becomes your standard, and people will follow your example.

Honesty is very simple. Tell the truth. Of course, sometimes we face obstacles in trying to be truthful. The truth is painful at times, so consider a person's feelings. Find a way to ease the blow. If you can't find a nice way of telling the truth, politely say, "I would rather not say."

Most of the time, being honest in our everyday lives is not so dramatic or sticky. Honesty means being a person of your word, not lying, not being deceptive through omission or commission. It is an everyday personal choice. It can be tough to do sometimes, but it will always make you feel good, and you will know you are doing the right thing. People respect honest people. They trust honest people. Honesty should be a standard for yourself.

Unfortunately, we don't always run into honest people. Dishonest people do not meet your standards. You can lead by example and hope they follow suit, but it is hard to keep a dishonest person close to you because of the unforeseen negative effects of their behavior. Cut a dishonest person loose from your circle of friends.

Both honesty and consideration show your respect for yourself and the people around you. Again, demanding respect from people does not mean disrespecting or belittling them. A disrespectful behavior, such as pushing aside a person on the street without saying, "Excuse me," may cause fear or tension and not respect. Respect comes from within and shines outward to the rest of the world.

Saying, "Excuse me," "Please," and "Thank you," is a common courtesy that should be shown to everyone and should not be rationed out based on rank, status, or familiarity. Showing respect reveals a level of respect you have for yourself; therefore, you can share it with the rest of the world.

The Drama Queen and the Bad News Bearer

Much as we don't like bad things to happen to us or to other people, they happen. People get into car accidents, relationships end, and sometimes we spill coffee or wine on our favorite outfits. Life is tough, but you don't have to make a fuss out of it every day or every weekend. Eventually, your friends will get tired of hearing about your bad luck, whether it is real or exacerbated by your need for attention.

There are two types of *drama queens*: *depressing drama queen* and *overreaction drama queen*.

Depressing Queen

A *depressing queen* wears her every painful emotion on her sleeve so that someone can rescue her from her pain or at least listen to her sorrowful story. She feels pain just like the rest of us, but she wants the world to know about every rip and tear in her heart and in her dress. This behavior is deflective. It may work for a moment, but eventually, people will get tired of her stories and assume the drama queen's woeful bad luck will befall them as well, thus staying away from her.

A depressing drama queen needs attention and goes about it the wrong way. The best attention springs from positive actions. If you feel sad about a breakup, ask a friend to do volunteer work with you or join a club. Helping people who are less fortunate feel good about themselves will make you feel good. You can learn something new. Wine or trapeze classes will get your mind off the doom and gloom and make you more interesting and fascinating to other people. Being fascinating and exhibiting leadership give you much attention, and you'll meet new people.

Death, divorce, breakups, and even bad days are part of our lives that we cannot change, and they are very painful. Take the time to focus and reflect. Call your friends and family, cry your eyes out, eat a tub of ice cream in your favorite sweats, but don't drag your baggage around for the world to see, hoping someone will come to save you from your pain. You can deal with your pain and find a way to move on. There are many professional and medical treatments for the pain that you cannot seem to deal with on your own. Seek them out so you can stop seeking the wrong attention.

HINT: If you have a depressing drama queen friend, politely pull her aside and let her know you are concerned about her well-being. But if she chooses to stay in the situation she is in, ask her to not share it with you anymore. It will be hard to be a true friend if you are drained with her problems she does not want to resolve.

Overreaction Drama Queen

An *overreaction drama queen*, or ODQ, is a scene-driven person. One thing goes wrong and she reacts in an exaggerated manner. A person bumping into her in a crowded club may set her off. A person wearing the same dress she is wearing at a function may cause a severe reaction from her. A local barista getting her coffee order wrong may turn a pleasant day into chaos. Being an ODQ is a more severe case of *drama* because the drama queen's actions are unpredictable and there is normally a prey. An ODQ may be reacting to a bad day, insecurity, or attention; or she may feel she is a victim of the world around her. Politely pull her aside and inform her that her behavior makes you feel uncomfortable. In today's world, situations like road rage, conflicts in nightclubs, and cruel treatment of classmates and coworkers often result in crimes and death. Don't keep company that can put your reputation and well-being at risk. Privately suggest anger management classes or self-esteem building activities, like exercise and mind and spirit workshops.

Bad news

Needless to say, no one likes bad news, so don't share it unless it is pertinent or an emergency and must be dealt with at that very moment. Only a gossiper and a troublemaker will present bad news about you or anyone else to the public. If you must be the bearer of the news, pull the person aside discreetly or have a one-on-one dialogue with him or her so she or he can deal with the issue directly or ask any questions without the prying eyes and ears around. Showing care and consideration will let that person (friend or foe) know that you have utmost respect for yourself and the people around you.

Everyday Manners

Social grace requires effort, and it must be practiced every day, which is normally uneventful, but it is a must in a civil society. The following are practical manners and courtesies we should all live by:

Entering and exiting elevators, mass transits, and buildings

Let people exit first, after which, you may enter. Hold the door for younger, elderly, and physically challenged people and allow them to enter first. If a young man is rude and whizzes by as you hold the door or enter, just let him rush in. You will look ridiculous if you try to beat him to the entryway. If someone is kind enough to hold the door for you, say, "Thank you."

Illness

Cover your mouth when you sneeze or cough; and then wipe, wash, or sanitize your hands. Always have a tissue or a handkerchief in your purse or pocket when you are sick. No one wants to hear your illness being sucked back up your nose or see it drain or wiped with your clothes and off your face.

Yawn

This is simple… Cover your mouth.

Giving up your seat in public transportation

Allow an elderly, pregnant, or physically challenged person to take a seat.

Cell Phone Use

Stay off your phone when placing an order face-to-face with a cashier; walking to your car alone (except if you are on the phone for safety reasons); dining; having a one-on-one talk with a friend; watching movies, theaters, and private shows; and attending parties. Cell phone use is distracting and takes your attention away from what you are currently doing, thus allowing mistakes and unsafe situations to arise. Using your cell phone while you are face-to-face with another person is rude and tells people around you that you would rather be somewhere else. If you must make a phone call, keep it short, quiet, and clean.

Appointments

Be five minutes early. Set your alarm or schedule five to ten minutes early so you can avoid being late. Being tardy is rude and gives the impression that you don't care about an event, a meeting, or a person.

Exiting into Moving Traffic

When exiting an escalator or a building, we often walk into the hustle and bustle of people on the move in front of or behind us. Step out of the way and keep moving in the direction you are going. You should always walk with purpose and briskness. Step aside, out of people's way, if you are lost or confused. Blocking exits of stores, buildings, and escalators is a safety hazard and is frustrating to people around you.

Planes

Upon entering a plane, put your luggage and belongings in the appropriate places (above in the overhead compartment or under the seat in front of you), and then immediately take your seat.

Don't rush to the bathroom when other passengers are trying to enter the plane and take their seats. The aisles are very narrow, and your behavior will only delay your flight. When your plane reaches the gate, wait for your turn to exit. Do not grab your belongings and rush to the exit. This only makes you look silly and immature.

Seating

Public places and public transportations may or may not have assigned seats. Be courteous and do not save seats if they are open to the public, like in many movie theaters and subways. Do not put wet umbrellas and other belongings on the seats next to you. Do not put your feet on the seats in front of you or on your sides. If you are saving a seat for a friend who is late or grabbing munchies in the lobby, inform people that the seat is taken. If you are alone, place your bags under your seat or on your lap so somebody can take the seats around you. Do not rush in to any place to get the perfect seat. Be cordial and take your time. Allow people ahead of you to enter first. If you are waiting for a seat to become available on a bus or a train, allow the person who has been standing or waiting the longest to take a seat first.

Gas

Gas happens to good people. When you are in a small and confined space, hold it until you get to a restroom or a private place. Do not burp. Wait until you get to a private place, or cover or close your mouth. Muffle the sound. Many people are sensitive to some smells and sounds, becoming nauseated with gross behavior. Keep your smells and sounds to yourself and in private. If you do have an accidental gas release, own up to it. Laughter and shock will last a moment; denial, on the other hand, will seem as though it will last a lifetime.

HINT: *Flying often causes gas, so keep foods that naturally make you gaseous to a minimum when flying.*

Eeewww Behavior

Do not dig, pick, or scratch any private part of your body or fissure in public. Do not perform in public any activity that is normally done in the privacy of your bathroom. If it is important that you check your appearance, go to the nearest restroom or powder room so you don't embarrass yourself and make people around you uncomfortable.

Technology

Keep cell phones, cameras, and other devices in your pocket or in your handbag when you are in public places where people assume a sense of privacy, like locker rooms, public restrooms and powder rooms, dressing rooms, spas, etc. Many gyms prohibit cameras or any items that can be used as a recording device because of the increased incidents of unauthorized picture taking. Such areas are private, and a cell phone or a camera can be used to record private moments. Many places request that you turn these devices off, but make it a habit for you to turn them off or keep them tucked away when you are in these places. The last thing you want is to see a person with a cell phone held in front of you as you change your clothes. Likewise, you don't want to make a person feel uncomfortable and assume that you will take inappropriate pictures of him or her.

Sound and Space in Public Places

Even in public places, people enjoy their personal spaces. It is very intrusive to invade other people's spaces by talking loud, walking or standing very close to them, playing loud music, or using the speaker on your audio devices. Mind the space and the people around you, and keep your life to yourself. Keep your voice low, and stand and walk about an arm's length away from people around you, if you can. You should hear music and other audios only through your earphones.

Personal Grace

Presenting yourself in the most positive way starts before you leave the house. Having a plan for each day and sticking to it allows you to stay on time and enjoy the day with a positive attitude and helps complete tasks.

Time Management

Write a list of tasks and goals to complete for the following day. Make sure the list is in a corner that is visible to you at the start of the day. You can have a list for your personal life and another for your work life.

Make a list of tasks for work and leave it at work on your desk. You can also plan your day the night before. Pick out your clothes the night before to avoid the dreaded "I have nothing to wear" complaint. Picking out your clothes early helps you plan your wardrobe according to your day's events, allowing you to get out of the house and be on your way early or on time. Lastly, set a schedule for your life. Set your alarm for your wake-up time and stick to it. Schedule your bedtime. Choose the time you would like to wake up, and then count backward seven or eight hours. That time should be your bedtime. Setting a regular bedtime schedule puts your body and mind at ease to rest and wake up refreshed.

Organize

Keep your living area clean and organized. Many of us have full-time jobs, families, and events to constantly tend to. Keeping everything in its place is a time management strategy and a must to stay organized. Running late for an appointment because you cannot find your shoes is unacceptable. On the other hand, arriving late to an appointment because you were at the doctor's office is understandable.

Money Management: A Small Leak Can Sink a Mighty Ship

Know your daily budget. Be honest with yourself about how much you can spend per day or per week. Having a savings plan keeps your future secure and makes everyday life more enjoyable because you don't have to worry about overspending. Break frivolous spending habits. We tend to buy minor items, like $5 coffee drinks, an extra nail polish, or snacks at lunch, when we could save a couple of dollars and accumulate a larger amount, which could be used for other must-haves or a more valuable purchase.

5

"Cutes good. But cute only lasts for so long, and then it's, 'Who are you as a person?' Don't look at the bankbook or the title. Look at the heart. Look at the soul. Look at how he treats his mother and what he says about women. And more important, how does he treat you? When you are dating a man you should always feel good." –
Michelle Obama

Dating

I love asking friends about their worst and best date stories. I always get an earful and a good laugh. When my turn to tell stories comes up, I realize I have more than enough bad date stories to share. I've had dates that told me their financial woes, had poor hygiene, and complained about their exes.

Yikes! But one of the worst dates I've ever had was a second date with a young man who bragged about kicking a woman out of his car (in the middle of nowhere) just because he didn't like her personality. I listened to his story with a shocked face and a bewildered question why he did not drive her back home rather than leave her on the side of the road. I thought to myself, *a gentleman would drive a woman back to her home.* Why this young man assumed his story would be entertaining to me, I haven't got a clue. I listened and learned that my date treated people the way he felt like treating them, regardless of their safety or his manners. Needless to say, I never saw that guy again. His lack of decorum and prideful boasting of disrespect made me question his future behavior toward me or anyone I knew. I could not see him as a friend or a mate.

Dating does not have to be as distressing as my story. It's supposed to be fun. Dating is seen by some as a way to meet people, have a great time, and hopefully meet the person of their dreams whom they can spend the rest of their lives with, or at the very least, make a lifelong friend. For others, it is a dreadful necessary means to an end: marriage. However you look at dating, what remains true is that it is a process that everyone must journey through in order to find a mate or have a relationship.

Have a positive outlook on dating. A date that results in a long romantic relationship is a plus. Start dating someone because you want to get to know him or her as a friend. Friends have an uncanny way of sticking around longer than the hot guy you met at the bar last week.

The techniques and etiquette of dating have evolved tremendously. You can meet and "date" online, you can have your friends set you up, you can join a singles club, you can become a member of a dating group, or the old-fashioned way, you can be approached by a person while you're out and about. If you want to date, try all avenues. Experimenting can be fun and rewarding. Just follow a few simple etiquette rules, be your best self, and stay safe. Your yearning for love should never outweigh your well-being and your safe return home to experience another day and another fun date.

The Art of Flirting

Every day we pass by hundreds of people we never notice. We rush to buy our groceries, get the paper, or play on our cell phones, never looking at people to say hello or give a smile of acknowledgment until we are in a bar or a club wanting to be noticed by someone. Take a breather. Stop! Smile! Take a moment to recognize the people around you. You might see a person who lights up your day. Start a conversation by mentioning the big game last night or the great weather. In a busy world, many people are simply happy a person notices they are alive. Each person you smile at or wish a great day may not be a great date or may never ask you out, but your short interaction with them will develop your habit of sharing a pleasant side of you, outside the matchmaking arena, and it's the first step in learning how to flirt.

Flirting is simple and can be non-intrusive. You don't have to drop a pencil and pick it up, bending at the hips or flipping your hair violently while biting on a drink stirrer. Subtlety is best, and men notice class acts. Make eye contact and smile. Most men notice a woman who is throwing glances to get attention.

If you are with friends, give a glance, smile, and gently laugh. Separate yourself from the pack a little so he will feel comfortable approaching. Do not go too far, such as outside the building. You want to stay safe. This person you are flirting with is a stranger, no matter how handsome he is. Go to the bar and get a drink, or walk to the powder room or to a shelf to check a book. He will notice your movement and take the chance to approach you without the audience of your friends. Men are nervous, sensitive, and scared of rejection, so they are more likely to approach when they can avoid being humiliated by his and your friends.

While cheerleading for the NFL, I would often pick a few people in the crowd to make eye contact with. When I would perform a sensual dance, I would think sensual thoughts. When I would make fun, active movements, I would think fun, active thoughts. I would take a quick glance and then move on to the next person. Eye contact and private thoughts kept the attention on me and made the interaction more interesting.

Create Sexual Energy

A technique taught by acting coach Ivana Chubbuck, of Ivana Chubbuck Studio, is sexual fantasy. Sexual fantasy is thinking sensual thoughts about another person. Actors use this technique when they meet a scene partner for the first time and they need to create sexual energy. In the dating world, think—do not share or act out—sexual fantasies when talking to your interest. Imagine your sexual positions, provocative areas, sensual sounds, etc., with your new interest. This technique allows you to forget about the nervous tension you may have and flirt with the pace and the sound of your voice and body movements. The person you are interested in will notice something but will not know what that "something" is.

Seductive versus Sleazy

Flirting to get attention is natural, whether you realize you are doing it or not. Some women giggle a little more, while others move and talk slower. Once we see a person who creates sexual attraction, our bodies' instincts kick in. Women also create ways to get attention, like undoing a top button to show a little cleavage, making a meal that her desired man will enjoy, or wearing the little dress he will love. These uncontrolled and carefully planned habits are called seduction.

Seduction is a wonderful and sometimes stressful part of life. Let it happen and enjoy, but don't turn a subtle seduction into a sleazy behavior. Today, reality shows take actions that are vulgar and self-destructive and present them as a positive way of life because we see them on television or splashed in the pages of magazines. The media gives sleazy behavior attention because it is abhorrent and unnatural. Flashing your breast in public, drinking more than what you can handle, pouring any liquid (water, liquor, juice) on yourself, or allowing someone else to pour it on you is sleazy. Men may be turned on for a moment, but such attention is short-lived. Ignore the reality show reenactments and be the lady men want to get to know rather than the woman they will try to avoid the morning after.

Have Standards

Set it a standard for a man to ask you out three days prior to the date. Expect him to make the plans, and inform him of any food or time restrictions you may have. Don't bend or change your standards so his behavior is acceptable.

If you don't go to a date that is scheduled on the same day that you are asked out and a man calls at the last minute, you should decline. Under certain circumstances, you can bend—for example, he wins concert tickets that day and wants to take you with him. Be reasonable, but don't be a doormat. Set rules, and he will follow them because he wants to be with you. If you must cancel the date, cancel as soon as possible and reschedule on the spot if you can. Unforeseen things happen; it's life. But thoughtless last-minute cancellations are rude and show a disregard for the other person, making you an unsuitable long-term mate.

Be Safe

Safety should be your first priority. Never give out your home address. Give your e-mail address instead of your home number. Take his information so you don't have to give your phone number, plus you can control the first couple of phone calls. You can still give your phone number and allow him to make the first call. Let him know if you prefer calling or text.

Date Like a Pro

The rules for dating have changed just as much as the rules of who approaches whom. Many women have strict rules about never asking a man to a date. If you do not feel comfortable asking a man out, don't, but know that you could be passing up a chance to meet a shy guy who might be the love of your life. If you do choose to make advances, you can approach a man without ever making him feel your testosterone levels are higher than his. A simple way to strike up a conversation with a man is to give a compliment. Give him a warm compliment on his outfit, his hair, or his physically fit appearance. We like compliments on our look, so do men. Don't compliment him on material things, like his watch, his car, etc., unless you have a good personal story to go with it. Giving material compliments is similar to a man complimenting you on your breast or your butt. You're going to think he just wants to sleep with you. Material compliments may lead him to believe you're materialistic. Once you got his attention, he may ask you out; if not, ask him out for a cup of coffee.

A coffee date is simple and easy to recognize if you want a real date with this person. If you get turned down, do not get upset; he might be taken. Tell him to have a great time the rest of his day and be excited that you took a risk. Greater risks get greater rewards.

If you are asking out a person whose contact information you already have, etiquette dictates that you ask three days ahead. Therefore, a Wednesday invitation is appropriate for a Saturday date. Make various date options for the person to choose from. Ask about any food allergies, religious restrictions, or time constraints when planning so your date will have the best time possible. Keep in mind that when you ask a person out, you cover the bill since you planned the date. Plan wisely and have fun.

Great boyfriends and husbands are like opportunities; none come knocking at your front door, so get out there and mingle.

The Last Man on Earth Syndrome

The last man on earth is the idea that this one guy you date has to lead to marriage. Always date multiple men. Men do it all the time. Have at least three men that you date regularly. Date them until you feel like you need to break-up or move forward with one person and have a solid commitment. The sad truth is, most of the men we date we will not marry. We may even hate their guts after a few months.

We normally date like so: We meet the guy. We like the guy. We devote our attention to this guy. After a couple of months, we want him to say he wants to be exclusive. After a year we want him to pop the question. If he does not, we get hurt and annoyed. Eventually we break-up. You spent two or more years in a relationship resulting in broken heart. We are back at the club, the networking event, asking friends about a new man and repeat until we find "the one." STOP!

Dating several men at one time will always make you a hot commodity that the man has to fight for your precious time. You will always know there are other fish in the sea. You will also avoid throwing all your eggs in one basket… if he is not ready to commit or more, you have John, Bob, and Joe knocking at your door.

When you act like you are a precious stone men believe it and you win.

HINT: *When dating, venture out and meet all kinds of people. Remember, a date may become a good friend, not just a romantic partner. Most friends outlast boyfriends.*

Date in Pairs

I don't mean a double date. Date a person twice before confirming or discarding the chances of a romantic connection. The first step is to know your standards for yourself, and then know the standards you have for the other person. Knowing your lifestyle makes it easy for you to know what you want in your life as well as what you can give the other person. Though you want the very best, it is in your best interest to be realistic. It is unfair to you, and to your date, to set a bar so high that only your dead grandfather could reach it in his heyday. It is also unfair to set rules that you do not follow for a prospective love interest. For example, it is unrealistic to want a person who is in shape and takes care of his or her body if you yourself have not set foot in a gym or worked out in over two years. Your standards should reflect your lifestyle and the rules you live by. If you are not looking for a person who lives by the standards you live by, you are setting up your relationship for failure.

Date 1

The first date should be short and sweet. Grab a cup of coffee, meet for happy hour drinks, or meet for brunch. Men may ask you to dinner and a movie, a park outing, or an event-filled day. These are wonderful outings for the second or third date, but not for the first. You are getting to know this person, so you want to have a chance to sit and discuss his hobbies, life, plans, etc., while you can actually listen and comprehend what he is saying. This gives you the chance to "read between the lines." Like most women, you want dates similar to those shown on ABC's *The Bachelor*; but you can be easily distracted by the glitz and the glamour of the events, the location, or the great dinner rather than truly learning more about the person you are letting into your life.

If you are the type of person who *needs* to do something to ease your nerves, by all means, do something fun and active, but you must know that the first date is about listening and sharing.

Plan an after-date activity with a friend. Plan to meet a friend at the zoo, have a lunch, or go on a shopping trip. Plan anything that will make you stick to ending the date after an hour or two. This gives you an out if the meeting is horrible, and you can bounce around the date experience with a friend who knows you and your lifestyle well. If you do not have a real out, make up one. Make plans for yourself to go about your day. You may not like your date after the first outing. If the date was horrid, it's okay. You only lost an hour of your life getting to know one person. If the meeting did not have sparks flying, plan to meet for a date one more time. It takes a couple of meetings to really get to know a person, so give it a chance.

Date 2

People are often nervous on the first date and make more mistakes than they would in their everyday lives, so give the person and yourself one more chance. The second date may be a little more relaxed because you are familiar with each other already and you can build upon your first meeting.

Meeting a person twice before judging a relationship allows you to get to know the person on the surface (hobbies, lifestyle, plans) on the first date, and then see if you make a good match based on your personalities, relationship standards, and plans on the second date.

Who Pays

In the past, a check was always placed in front of the man at the table, but today, it is placed in the middle of two people or at the edge of the table. This procedure eliminates the uncomfortable moment of passing or grabbing for the check. The proper etiquette is that the person who invited the other out should pay for the date. It is also proper manners to offer to pay for your meal when your date wants to grab the check. If you were asked out on a date, offer to pay for your meal, though it is proper for the person who planned and proposed the date to pay for everything. If the date planner accepts your offer, it is up to you if you want to date him again.

If you asked a person out on a date, you should pay for the date. Some men do not allow women to pay no matter what, so accept his offer and allow him to pay. Return the favor by sending him a thank-you gift. Sex is not a thank-you gift, and your body should not be a prize for paying for a meal.

Send him flowers, a thank-you card, or candy. Your gracious gesture will show respect for his money and his time. Some men feel comfortable paying, but they will appreciate being pampered. Plan a date where everything is previously paid for, or plan a picnic where all he has to do is show up and enjoy your company without having to lift his wallet or a finger. Your gratitude will be understood and respected.

Body Language

Dating can be a very intimidating experience. Many of us express anxiety through our bodies, though our voice may sound calm. Crossing our arms, biting our lips, picking our fingers, and slouching our shoulders are often manifestations of nervousness. Monitor your movements to get familiar with your body before the date. Crossing your arms is often seen as blocking a person from "entering" or getting to know you. Biting your lip and picking your nails are more noticeable nervous behaviors, and they mark your body, causing split and chapped lips or painful hangnails. Your date opposite you may notice this habit and see it as lack of confidence. If you notice that you are giving off bad body language, take a deep breath, exhale, smile, and correct your actions. Exhaling relaxes your muscles and allows you to show ease and confidence.

Letting Go

After the second date, you should have an idea what type of person your date is. If he is not the person you see yourself with, be honest with him and let him go. Inform him of your decision so he can continue dating and meeting other people.

Example: "John, it was lovely meeting you and getting to know you, but I think it is best we remain friends. I think you are a great guy, so I wish you all the luck in dating."

Be stern and don't hold back from telling the person you are not interested in him romantically or platonically. Do not hide behind bushes, trying to avoid a person and his phone calls. Respect him by letting him go gracefully and clearly so he can continue searching for the person of his dreams. He will respect you for your honesty.

If you don't feel a person is a good partner for you, he may be a great match for a friend or may turn out to be a good friend. Hold on to his card or information so you can pass it along or invite him to large events to meet your other friends.

If your relationship has gone beyond two dates and you want to end the relationship, meet the person in a public place. Let him know your differences and explain that it is best that you part ways. Be stern. Be clear. And be warm. Understand that he may be hurting, but don't give him mixed messages to ease the blow of the breakup. It will only prolong his pain. Do not send a text, an e-mail, or a Post-it (à la *Sex and the City*). Whether you think that person deserves to hear your voice or not, you need to be the bigger person and the respectful one. Calling after the second date or meeting after several dates to break up also eliminates any confusion in ending the relationship.

A Relationship Blossoms

After the first few dates, the fun begins because you are both relaxed and comfortable with each other already. You will get to know him and have the honor of meeting his closest friends and family. It will be an honor to meet his family, as it will be an honor for him to meet your close friends and family.

Treat the situation as such. Don't use vulgar language, even if his family and friends cuss like sailors. Don't do it. Don't wear clothes that will make a person ask if you are on your way to perform at the strip club or round up a few pigs in the yard. Be your best self. Look clean, together, and relaxed. Read the paper to brush up on current events and have a couple of topics you want to talk about that are positive and not controversial. Do not gossip, ask personal or financial questions, make any sexual jokes or references about you and your date, or put on an air of elitism. Be yourself. Know what characteristics make you special, and let those characteristics shine.

Just as you plan how you want his friends and family to perceive you, put the same amount of care and effort in introducing your new beau to your family and friends. Introduce your new love with accolades. Do not share the details of his job, financial standing, or resume. Allow your date to divulge his personal information when he feels comfortable. Prompt your date to discuss his hobbies, his education, and the current events that he cares about and has knowledge of. Share similarities he may have with your family members and friends.

This puts your new significant other on steady ground and gives him room to grow and become friends with the people you hold dear. Your date will also notice you have been listening to everything he has said, and you will have his best interest in mind.

Don't Get too Comfortable

Many people become very set in their ways once a relationship has begun a steady pace, allowing good manners and etiquette to fade away. This can be seen as the bait and switch. Don't change your personality once you have your love's interest, stick to the same standards. Don't take calls during dinner, or take your phone out during dinner or every time he is around. Shower and look your best every day. Do not use vulgar language, attack his views, or downplay his efforts or feelings now that he is smitten. Always give him your best because you want nothing less from him.

Body Movement and Poise

While modeling on *The Price Is Right*, I had to climb in and out of beds, cars, boats, chairs . . . and trampolines. The nerve-racking part of the job was never about missing my mark onstage. Anxiety would set in when I had to make everyday movements into eye-catching fun yet sensual moves. I created simple movements that increased the sensuality of mundane tasks. I made these moves while being surrounded by a crew of men, a large audience, and cameras at every angle. Proper poise and movement will help you exit cars, climb out of bed, or simply sit on a chair with grace, poise, and a touch of sexual flair. The key is keeping your legs together at the knees. Pinch any short skirts and shorts on the sides, away from sight, to prevent fabric rise. Let go once standing upright.

HINT: Don't over think your moves and position. Relax and have fun.

Lying in Bed

Always lie on your side with the bottom leg extended and the other leg slightly bent with toes softly pointed. Be sure to lie on your hip or tilt your body a little toward the front, letting the knee fall on the bed. This position gives your body curve.

Walking

Walk with your hips and with an intended direction, one foot in front of the other. Don't swing your hips too much; you would look as though you're trying to be sexy. When walking from the bed, touch your hip or swing your hair to shake it out. A little movement distracts the eyes of the viewer.

Sitting Up in Bed

Bend both or one leg up. Prop your pillows up behind you and rest one arm on the pillow beside you. Do not lay both legs together in front of you. It gives an image of a wide mass of skin and fat.

Climbing Out of Bed (or Car)

Swing both legs over the edge of the bed. Do not climb out of the bed with one leg on the floor and the other leg in bed. You will give a big crotch shot.

Lying on Your Stomach Naked

Prop the pillow under your chest between your arms so your breasts get a lift and a rounded shape. Arch your back slightly to lift and round your bottom. Your butt and breasts have curve rather than appearing flat and sloppy.

Let's Talk about SEX . . .

No one should tell you when you should become intimate with someone. The decision to have sex is your choice. You say where, when, and how.

No Means No

When you decide not to have sexual intercourse with a person or perform any intimate act, *be clear and stern*. If you imply that you are irresolute, either through body language or through words, the person might believe there is a chance for a sexual encounter if he continues to persuade you to change your mind. Let him know you like him but you are not interested in or not ready for an intimate relationship.

Example: John: "Let's take this to the room."

Sue: "John, I'm really interested in getting to know you, but I'm not ready to become intimate with you. Maybe in the future when our relationship is deeper."

Let's Get it On

Sex is exciting, wonderful, and scary. We tend to revert to our insecure selves, wondering if we were good, if our butts are too big or to small, or if he saw the inverted nipple or the stretch marks. Sex exposes our most intimate parts . . . literally, but we don't have to succumb to anxiety and insecurities. Confidence is key! At night, dim the lights so he can only see small sections of your body when the light hits your curves. The room is dim, so strut like a movie star sex symbol toward the bed. Don't run! Fake confidence until you believe it. Your partner wants to be there, with you. Make it clear you want to be there, at that moment, with him.

Look Fly When You Rise and Shine

Getting out of bed can be pretty tricky if you don't feel confident with your physical appearance. No, you cannot wrap the sheet around you and leave your lover cold in the bed. If you can muster the confidence to stand up and walk to the bathroom to freshen up completely naked, do it. It shows you have control and confidence.

Some of us need a little help getting out of bed. Here are a couple of tricks. Slowly stretch and gaze in his direction. If he is still asleep, look around the room for a shirt of his on the floor or close to the bed. If you find a shirt, slowly rise from the bed with a bigger stretch, running your hands through your hair to loosen any knots or for a quick style fix. Plant your feet on the ground and have your back facing your lover. If you find a shirt, put it on. If you find an unused blanket, gracefully reach for it and wrap it around your body. Get up and go to the bathroom. If you cannot find an article of clothing or a blanket, simply get up and walk to the bathroom with the same strut you walked to get to bed. Do not use your hands to hide your private parts; he has already seen it, touched it, and grabbed it. He knows your body, so be confident. He will love your poise.

If your new lover is wide-awake, you can sit on the edge of the bed, at least one foot planted on the floor. If your back is turned toward your mate, give a slight turn from your waist to your head, and keep your back straight. This angle will give more curves to your waistline and prevent your body from giving a tired slouch.

HINT: *You should always have an overnight kit. Keep a travel-size toothbrush, a face wash, hairpins, a deodorant, a moisturizer (it will help clean smudged makeup and tame stray hair), and a change of panties with you. You can fit everything into a plastic sandwich bag or a mini toiletry bag.*

You're Dumping Me?

If you are on the receiving end of a breakup, listen and accept it. Most of us experience a breakup in some form or fashion, but you can walk away with your head held high. Ending a relationship and possibly losing a friend is hard to take when you feel it came out of nowhere, so listen and ask a couple of questions to fully understand why your partner feels a certain way and how he came to his conclusion. The information he gives isn't necessarily a fact about you. Don't run out and change your wardrobe only because he wants to see your legs and you don't own a miniskirt. Don't begin a bodybuilding routine because this guy prefers female body builders. Politely thank him for the time you shared and wish him luck.

Do not e-mail, text, Facebook, YouTube, call, tweet, etc., only to stay in contact with him. Do not beg for reconciliation or for further understanding after the initial breakup. Do not get friends—yours or his—involved to look for understanding from him or to assist you in clarification from him. You *should* have your friends to cry with or play a game of pin the tail on the donkey (with his face as the donkey, of course).

Breakups hurt, but they are also a new beginning and a learning experience. Walk away a lady. He will miss you and respect you more, even if you never talk to him again. My advice... Join a club to experience a new phase of your life, redecorate your room, or buy new lingerie. Do not share your anger, sad feelings, or painful stories for the world to read on the Internet or on social networks. Talk to a person whom you trust in order to receive comfort. One day, you will meet somebody whom you will love and who will love you back. The last thing you want is for your new love to see how you crumbled over your last man.

Never air your dirty laundry in public. A moment of comfort from online friends equals a lifetime of reliving a breakup and a broken heart. What you write online is online permanently.

A woman who airs her dirty laundry in public for all to see is opening her life to be judged by people who only know half of the story. Know your value, and have your standards. Accept the breakup and gather the strength to move on and find a person who is perfect for you. The last thing you want is to find Mr. Right and then explain your crazy reactions and emotions about a previous breakup. Make a clean break so you can have a fresh start with your new life and your potential new love.

Mending a Broken Heart

Why run after a man who shows you he does not care for you? Man can show his not interested in pursuing a relationship with you before the first date, on the third date, or after two years. The following tips will help you mend your broken heart and start over again.

- Join a local club or social group
- Erase all of his contact information to avoid drunken calls and text.
- Go to the gym- Working out helps cleat the mind and your body benefits
- Plan fun girl night out events
- After some much needed alone time and soul searching, start a "Say Yes" plan. Whenever anyone asks you to do something new or for a date say "YES!"

6

"You are what you eat, so don't be FAST, CHEAP, EASY or FAKE." –Unknown

Dining

I have always loved good food, so eating almost everything on my plate is not uncommon for me. When I was very young, I did not know dining etiquette as much as I know today. One day, my class had cereal for our early-morning breakfast. As I neared the bottom of the bowl, I picked the bowl and put it to my mouth. I began to slurp and drink from the bowl, enjoying the remaining cereal and milk. The teacher, almost in shock, tapped my arm and informed me that people don't eat that way. I had to use a spoon like a respectable little girl.

As I matured, I learned more about dining and appropriate dining manners. I was also able to differentiate casual dining from more upscale events and fine dining. Like most young girls who played tea party and dress-up, I enjoyed elegant dining because I could put on a beautiful dress and a great pair of my mother's heels. Attending an elegant affair excites me. I get to wear a lovely dress and alluring jewelry and imagine I am a princess with all the fixings—except a crown, of course. Playing dress-up is fun, but once you step into a room with tables dressed as elegantly as you are, the etiquette of eating, sipping, and simply sitting can be daunting. Arm yourself with proper dining etiquette, and you will feel comfortable in any situation.

Seating

The first step is finding your place. If you are attending a hosted event, you may have assigned seating. The host would (and should) have put a lot of thought into who sits where and next to whom, so don't ask to change your seat, and do not take it upon yourself to sit where you feel most comfortable in. Sit wherever you please if seats are not assigned.

Name cards are placed on the table in front of the event entrance or on your table setting. Many large events have a table outside the dining area with name cards. Each card will have a guest's name and a table number. Take your card and walk to the table, or let the host help find your seat. If you are entering a restaurant, go to the host stand and inform them of your party's arrival and they will seat you. If you are meeting a party that is already seated, tell the hostess and he or she will walk you to the table and seat you. The host will pull out your chair for you to take a seat.

Some men stand, and one of them pulls out your chair for you to sit, but today's society is very informal and lacks knowledge of some etiquette and chivalry, so do not be offended if this does not happen. Do not wait for men to stand and pull out your chair. If they do not do it, simply seat yourself. If your chair is pulled out for you, take your seat from the right side of the chair. Grab your chair on the side or from behind to push forward and guide the seat under you. During this process, the person who pulled out your chair will assist you. Thanking him for the assistance and nodding at the men for their respect should express your gratitude. Acknowledgment goes a long way.

Leaving the table to take a call, powder your nose, or do any other temporary exit does not need assistance or acknowledgments. The constant movement would be too distracting and uncalled-for. You should excuse yourself without explaining further what you are going to do and then return and seat, never disturbing the rest of the party. No one needs to know you have to go to the bathroom; you must take this important call from so-and-so, etc. Say, "Please excuse me," place your napkin on your chair, and tend to your business. When you return, seat yourself, place your napkin back on your lap, and carry on with the evening.

Table Settings

Table settings can seem overwhelming when your number one goal is to enjoy the food and the company. Your bread plate, water glass, and salad fork will be easy to locate once you understand and practice these simple etiquette rules.

A place setting has a dinner plate, salad plate, bread plate, water glass, a wineglass (white, red, or both), salad fork, dinner fork, dessert fork or dessert spoon, soup spoon, salad knife, dinner knife, butter knife, and a napkin. A table made for informal dining or evening supper will have fewer utensils and glasses.

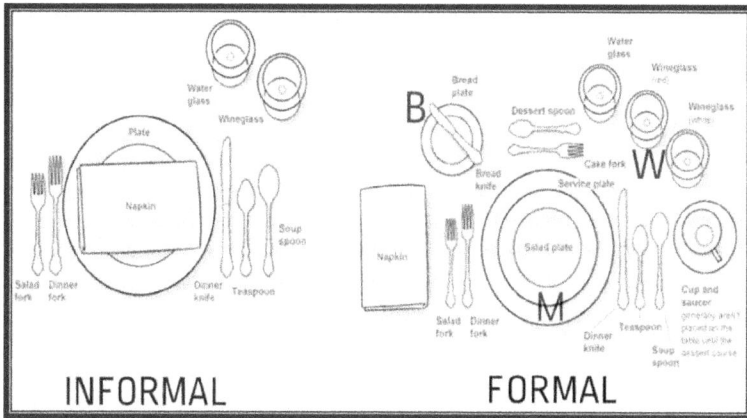

The diagram shows consistency in flatware and glass placements in both the formal setting and the informal setting. A full table can be confusing, and you do not want to grab another guest's glass of water or fork. Your drinking glasses are always on your right, and your fork is always on your left. A code for your plate setting on the table is BMW (*b*read on the left, *m*eal in the middle, and *w*ater/wine on the right). Knowing where your utensils, drinking glasses, and plates are will keep your hands and mouth on your items only.

Formal and informal dining settings are placed by course within the meal. Most casual restaurants offer a three-course meal: appetizer, dinner, and dessert. A more formal restaurant or event may offer a five-course meal: appetizer or soup, fish, salad, main course, and dessert. In many cultures, the salad may be served after the dinner and the appetizer is a separate course from the soup. Most Westernized meal practices place the salad before the main course. For each course served, your table setting will have a utensil to use. Your utensils are placed by course from the outside in. Therefore, if the appetizer is soup, you will have a soup spoon farthest from the plate on your right side. Your second course is normally a fish. You will have a fish fork, a cocktail fork, or an oyster fork farthest from your plate. The oyster fork, which is used for shellfish, may be placed on the right side, next to the spoon. The salad is the next course, followed by the main course, and then the dessert.

Utensils and Stemware

When dining out, a table will have the standard flatware and drinking glasses (view informal place setting), but depending on what the host or restaurant is serving, several setting items may not be present and some may be added.

It is always good to arm yourself with knowledge of every item and its use rather than be thrust into a situation and not know the difference between a cocktail fork and a dinner fork. Below are the utensils and stemware you may use.

Forks

Dinner fork. The largest fork with four tines. This fork is used for the main course.

Salad fork. A four-tine fork and similar to the dinner fork, but it is shorter and may have wider-spread tines.

Fish fork. The fish fork has three tines and is similar in length to the salad fork.

Lobster fork. This is a narrow long-stemmed, two-tine fork. The structure allows the user to remove meat from lobster and crab shells. The lobster fork is accompanied with a lobster cracker.

Oyster fork. A small fork used for shellfish. It has two tines and is very narrow.

Cocktail fork. A fork that is narrow and as small as or smaller than the oyster fork. It has three tines and is often used for appetizers due to its small size.

Spoons

Soupspoon. There are two types of soupspoons: the standard soupspoon and the bouillon spoon. The standard soupspoon has many uses. The *bouillon spoon*, on the other hand, is only used for bouillon and other light soups.

Bouillon spoon. A round deep bowl to scoop the broth of the soup with ease.

Standard soupspoon. A shallow and narrow bowl. Soupspoons can be used for scooping heavier soups and stews and for assisting in controlling the amount of pasta on your fork, sauce, fruit, and sometimes dessert.

Caviar spoon. Unlike other spoons, caviar spoons are made of mother-of-pearl, wood, or gold. Silver alters the taste of caviar. This spoon is very small and only used for placing caviar on your portion of food. This spoon is for serving only.

Teaspoon. Smaller than the dessertspoon and soupspoon. It is used for stirring and sipping tea and coffee.

Espresso or demitasse spoon. Another very small spoon used for cappuccino and espresso. The spoon fits the small structure of the espresso cup and saucer.

Dessertspoon. The dessertspoon has many uses. It is the most common size of spoon in most households and restaurants. It is used with cereal, desserts, and tea.

Iced tea and ice cream spoon. The long handle and the small bowl allow the user to stir content in a standard glass or an ice cream glass.

Knives

Informal steak knife. A casual steak knife normally has a wooden or plastic handle. This knife is used to cut red meat. Most entrées with meat are normally paired with vegetables. Use the steak knife to cut both types of food rather than changing knives.

Formal steak knife. A more upscale restaurant or a special event has a steak knife with a metal handle beveled similar to the fork and spoon settings.

Dinner knife. The dinner knife is the most common knife. The table knife is rounded and used to cut poultry and seafood such as shrimp, scallops, octopus, etc., excluding fish. The dinner knife is also used to cut any other food on your plate.

Butter knife. This cutlery is smaller than the dinner knife and rounded on both sides. The butter knife is only used for cutting butter and spreading it on your bread. Do not cut the bread with your knife. You should break the bread with your hands and then spread the butter with your knife.

Fish knife. Fish during the main course is the only kind of food that the fish knife should be used on. The tip of the knife is pointed with a blade on the left side and grooves or notches on the right. The point and blade are to assist in cutting meat from between the bones. The notched side of the knife is to help lift and remove the bones from the meat.

Entremets knives. These knives are smaller than the dessertspoon and the fork. One knife is wide and rounded at the top. It is used for dessert that has crust or bread. The narrower knife has a sharper point and a sharper blade. This knife is used for salad or cheese served after dinner.

Stemware and Glasses

An upscale event can have up to five glasses on a table, positioned with the smallest and the water goblet in front and the other three behind them arranged according to height. The bar may offer you another type of glass, depending on the drink or the cocktail. Below are a few of the styles you may use and want to stock in your own bar.

Water goblet. Used for water. Some restaurants or events have two water goblets available. One is for water, and the other is for juice or iced tea.

Champagne flute. A tall slender glass used for champagne. Champagne is served chilled and should stay very cold. The bowl of the flute allows the bubbles to glide down the sides, toward the center, and then rise from the middle of the glass. This keeps the champagne fresh. Hold the glass at the stem, away from the base of the bowl, to avoid warming the champagne for longer enjoyment. The coupe glass was more popular during the 1920s and earlier and is rarely used today because of spillage and loss of flavor and. Fill the glass bowl no more than halfway.

White wine glass. The glass is tulip-shaped with the top of the glass narrow and the base wide. White wine is served chilled, so hold the stem with your fingers and your thumb away from the bowl.

Red wine glass. Red wine is served warm in a stemmed glass with a large bowl. A Burgundy glass has a larger bowl for maximum exposure to air. It is okay to hold the glass around the bowl or on the stem.

Liqueur or cordial glass. This glass looks like a smaller cone-shaped wineglass and stands about four inches tall. Often used for dessert or after-dinner wines. Liqueur glass bowls come in many shapes and, therefore, can be held by the bowl or the stem.

Martini. The martini glass has a wide-shaped cone, and martini is served cold. Hold the stem close to the base of the bowl to avoid spilling the top-heavy glass. Some people hold the top of the glass because of the wide mouth, but this warms the martini faster.

Shot glass. A short 1.5 oz. drinking glass used for potent alcoholic drinks. Base of glass is thick due to the common practice of slamming the glass on a bar after consuming the drink.

Pilsner glass. The classic beer glass. In many casual atmospheres like in bars, tailgating, and barbecues, beers are enjoyed from the bottle. When you opt for a glass, use a beer mug or a pilsner glass to keep your beer chilled.

Highball. A tall tumbler used for drinking cocktails, sodas, and fruit drinks.

Tumbler or double old-fashioned. This is a short wide glass used for drinking straight alcoholic drinks. Many restaurants use this glass for mixed cocktails as well.

Brandy snifter. The brandy snifter has a wide and large bowl on top of a short stem. Brandy is served warm; therefore, cupping the glass from underneath the bowl at the top of the stem helps preserve the heat.

HINT: The pinky is normally free to relax when you hold most glasses.

Do not stick your pinky out. It is seen as pretentiousness and is often a gag to show "high society" standards. Keep the pinky relaxed and close to the other fingers.

Enjoy Your Dinner

You have now taken your seat, and you are ready to dig in to a wonderful meal. As previously mentioned, you should not be starving when you arrive at the party. Have a bite before you get there. This saves you from stuffing your face when you should be resting your fork and talking. Eating beforehand also lessens the hunger for the rest of the night in case you do not care for the food being served.

Eating Styles

There are two types of eating styles when it comes to holding your fork and knife: Continental and American. American is the most common style used in the United States, while Continental is used in most of the other parts of the world. Familiarize yourself with both, but once you are at an event and you begin eating, stick to one type of eating style for the entire meal.

American

Hold the fork with your right hand with tines facing upward and the knife with the left hand. Your right hand is normally stronger, so when you must cut an item, switch the fork to the left hand (tines facing up) and the knife to the right. Proceed to cut your food, and then switch utensils back to begin eating. It is perfectly acceptable to use your knife to assist in placing food on your fork.

Continental

Hold your fork in the left hand, tines facing down toward the plate. The fork also faces downward while transporting food from the plate to your mouth.

Your knife is in your right hand. For both cutting and eating, your fork and knife stay in the designated hands. The Continental style of dining allows you to use your knife at ease to assist food on the fork and cut.

Hold your fork in the left hand, tines facing down toward the plate. The fork also faces downward while transporting food from the plate to your mouth. Your knife is in your right hand. For both cutting and eating, your fork and knife stay in the designated hands. The Continental style of dining allows you to use your knife at ease to assist food on the fork and cut.

Take a Breather

Resting your knife and fork is universal. Place the handle of your knife at five o'clock on your plate close to the edge and place your fork handle at eight o'clock, close to the edge as well. For the American fork resting position, the tines face up, while for the Continental position, the tines face down. If you're eating soup, rest your spoon handle at three o'clock.

By placing your utensils in the right position when you are still eating, the waitstaff would be aware that you are still eating and know not to remove your plate. Do not place your fork, knife, or spoon on the table after you have started using it; it should remain on your plate or in your bowl.

Finished!

At the end of the meal, American and Continental styles also differ: The American style places the fork and the knife side by side at a five o'clock position with tines down, while the Continental signal for "finished" is similar to its resting style, except you cross the top portion of the fork and the knife. If you are eating soup, take the spoon out of the bowl and place the spoon across the top of the plate the bowl is sitting on. If your soup bowl does not have a plate beneath it, leave the spoon in the resting position. Place your napkin on the left side of your plate to signal to the waitstaff that you have finished your meal.

Mind your Manners and your Dinner Mates

There are some things we do by habit, and we fail to think what our actions mean. Be aware of these habits and break them. Burping, eating with your mouth open, and talking with your mouth full are all habits that are not appropriate whether in the privacy of your home or in public.

Little Notes and No-no's

Do not point the blade of the knife outward, toward another guest. It is not only unsafe, as it may cut the other guest, but also seen as a sign of hostility.

If your utensil falls to the floor, do not pick it up and place it on the table. Signal the waitstaff with a glance to remove it and give you a new one.

Pass all food served family style to the right, allowing a person to take the handle of the serving dish. When you have the bread bowl first, offer bread to the person on your left, and then take one for yourself and pass the bowl to your right.

Trained Staff Know

Every restaurant trains its staff to serve you best. Know the correct signals to give and what you should avoid.

Snapping your fingers at anyone is rude. Never raise your hand, snap your fingers, clap, or yell at member of the waitstaff. A person who treats people as though they are beneath him or her is not worthy of any service or friends. Use eye contact. A trained waiter continuously checks on his dinner guests and will respond.

Close the menu once you have decided on what you want to order. A waiter comes to take the order after the menu is closed. If you keep the menu open, it is a sign that you are still looking and undecided. A waiter will give you time to view the menu without disturbance, so close the menu when you are ready.

If your waiter is not responding as quickly as you would like him or her to do, contact another waiter to send your waiter over. If the service is terrible, quietly excuse yourself from the table and talk to a manager or a maître d'. Making a scene to get a better service will give you the complete opposite.

Do not stack plates, hand dirty items to the waiter, or clean the table or plates for her or him. Bussing staff and waiters have a uniform process for clearing your table; allow them to do so.

Ordering a drink at a crowded bar can be tricky. Most bar areas are very crowded, and the bartenders are doing their best to attend to everyone's needs. To make sure you get your order in a timely manner, politely make your way to the front of the bar. Look for an opening or slide next to a person who is receiving his drink. Eye contact is important at the bar as well. A smile goes a long way too. As soon as the bartender walks over to you or is finishing a drink for the person beside you, tell him or her your order fast and directly. Most of all, be patient; she or he will serve you as soon as he or she can.

Salt, Pepper, Soy Sauce, Hot Sauce, Etc.

Don't dowse your food with these seasonings until you have tried your food. You may be pouring salt on an item that is already salty. At a dinner party, this is seen as very rude to the host. Try the meal first before you to "adjust" it. Once you have possession of the salt and pepper, always pass the salt and pepper together, even when asked for just one of the two.

YUCK! To send or not to send food back?

Many chefs and restaurants prepare a meal for you that you may not be pleased with. It could be the presentation; the cream sauce when you thought the sauce should be tomato, or a rare steak when you've ordered well-done. The appropriate thing to do is to try the food and see if you like it the chef's way rather than your way. You may find a new favorite. If you get a meal that is edible but not your favorite, find a way to enjoy it. Eat the side items of the meal, and eat around the undesired portion.

If your entrée is completely inedible, such as when a huge fly makes your mashed potatoes its final resting place, or a chicken meal arrives and you are a vegetarian, let the waiter know immediately and send the food back. Be polite and discreet. Inform the rest of the party to continue eating. Do not return food just because you don't like the chef's choice to grill the steak rather than broil it. The restaurant or chef is not interested in a cooking lesson from you. Sending your food back to the kitchen often causes a twenty-minute delay for the other patrons in the restaurant. Return food only when you cannot eat it. If it is just a minor item, like a shred of cheese (and you don't have cheese on your meal) or any other non-deadly foreign object, simply remove it without a fuss.

Complaints

An easy way to complain about the food or the service is to attach a compliment. I call it the *Complaint Sandwich*. Give the restaurant or the entrée a compliment, give your complaint, and then end with another compliment.

Example: "Sir, I always order the salmon here and I love it, but today the salmon is burned and the rice is undercooked. This restaurant is one of my favorites, so I would love to order something different."

Most management staffs are more willing to help people who give them compliments and do not act aggressively or complain excessively.

Finishing Dinner

You are not a child. You do not have to finish everything on your plate. Some meals are so delicious that you want to finish them all, but avoid scraping the plate or using your bread to soak up every bit of sauce or gravy. It is fine to use your bread to place the last bit of food on your fork. It is also acceptable to use your knife in this process. Using your bread allows you to enjoy a little more of the meal after the main contents are devoured. When your meal is complete, place your utensils in the "finished" position.

To Drink or Not to Drink

Alcohol is the one option on the menu that can either keep a wonderful night going or destroy a good time. Be cautious. Alcohol impairs your judgment, so order an alcoholic beverage only if you can handle a drink or two. If you do not have tolerance for alcohol, it is perfectly fine to drink club soda or any other nonalcoholic beverage.

You should only order a drink if the host orders a drink for herself or himself. If you are with your boss or an authority figure, order a drink only if your superior orders an alcoholic drink, you are not discussing money or pertinent business matters, or it is not lunch. You want to be alert and give your guest or host your attention, not the sorority party version of yourself. Remember, keep your drinking maximum to two drinks even if you can gracefully talk and walk after six drinks, lest people around you will start questioning your character and judgment. Save the college-style drinking for girls' night out.

A Conversation Piece

Always keep the conversation clean (refer to chapter 2). Your conversation at the dinner table should always be about everyday events. Arm yourself with the headlines of the day and topics you would like to discuss should the conversation wane. Never discuss any topic that you would talk about in the bedroom or the bathroom.

Dinner and Dating

Many of the etiquette rules and manners discussed previously apply to dining with a person you have a romantic interest in. The difference is that it is an intimate scenario.

Drinking

Drinking on a date is a delicate situation. Alcoholic beverages give a feeling of relaxation by suppressing your natural defenses. Dating can cause anxiety and stress, but safety comes first. Order only one drink during the first few dates. Sip the wine or alcoholic cocktail so it will last long, and drink plenty of water while dining.

This allows you to enjoy the meal and not worry about your impaired judgment toward the end of the evening. A clear mind allows you to stay safe and shows your dinner guest you are definitely having a good time without overindulging and losing control.

Conversation

Sex is never a good topic on a first date. Never bring it up, and change the subject once your date starts talking about it. Inform him you would like to get to know him outside the bedroom. You want a person to get to know your hobbies, your likes and dislikes in life, and your childhood quirks. If your date is more interested in what's your favorite position than what your favorite movie is, he probably is not interested in sticking around to get to know *you*.

Ordering

It is rude to order the most expensive item on the menu on a date or in any social gathering where you are not picking up the tab. Order an item of equal or lesser value than your date's or the host's, unless your date insists that you order that particular item which happens to be the most expensive.

Eating Complicated Food

Crab

Twist the legs at the joint closest to the body to remove the legs. Break the crab legs at the joints. This will allow the meat to become loose so you can use your seafood fork to pull the meat from the shell. If you do not have the ability to remove the meat from the joints, break the center of the shell with a seafood cracker and remove the meat. After removing the legs from the body, turn the body of the crab upside down and remove the apron (a tab in the center of the body). Slowly separate the top half of the crab from the bottom, as though you are opening a sandwich. Once open, you will see the "mustard" or the "junk." Remove this portion and enjoy the meat underneath with your seafood fork. In a more casual setting, it is fine to use your fingers to remove the meat. Many people use wooden mallets to crack the shell of the body and the legs. Do so with caution. Tap the shell just enough to crack the shell. This process prevents you and other guests from being hit by crab pieces. The shell breaks into small pieces, so avoid taking them in by picking away all the shell parts before eating. Place all discarded shells in the bowl or bucket provided, or on the side of your plate.

Lobster

Like the crab, you must remove the claws from the body of the lobster by twisting the claws at the joint closest to the body. Hold the body down on the plate, and then twist the claws off the body. Use the seafood cracker to crack the claws, and then remove the meat with your seafood fork. Next, remove the tail from the body by turning the lobster upside down so the belly is exposed. Twist the tail until it is removed from the body. Place the body aside for consumption or discard it. Use a knife to cut the underside of the tail, and remove the meat, or use your fork to pull out the meat from the open portion of the tail. Locate the digestive tract (a black vein-like substance), remove and discard.

Some people do not eat the body of the lobster, but it is edible, though it has less meat and "junk" that you may remove or eat. Cut an opening in the belly of the body. You can use a seafood cracker or a knife. You will see some meat and a greenish substance (tomalley for female lobsters) or a reddish substance (roe for male lobsters). This is where the brains and intestines are located; these are edible and considered as a delicatessen, but some people do not eat them.

Pick out the meat and the portions you choose to eat with a fork and discard the rest. Lastly, the legs can be removed from the body by twisting the legs off and removing the meat with a seafood fork. In a more casual setting, you may use your fingers. The legs do not contain much meat, so fussing with the lobster legs in more formal settings may be distracting, and your time will be better served complimenting your host or date.

Shrimp and Prawns

Most high-end establishments serve shrimp with the shell removed. Shrimp may also have the tail shell on while the body is removed. Hold the shrimp down with your fork and cut the tail off with the knife.

Casual restaurants serve prawns and shrimp with the shell on, so you have to remove the shell with your hands. Hold the shrimp belly side up with one hand; use the other hand to bend the head of the prawn back until it snaps off. Discard or place the head on the side of your dish. Use your free hand to pull back the shell and the legs of the prawn in a downward motion. Your thumb will force the shell to slide off easily, including the tail. If the tail remains attached, tug on the tail shell, and it will slide off or break off the body. Discard the shell in the bucket or bowl provided. If a bowl is not available, place the shell on the side of your plate.

Soup

The most important rule on eating soup and all meals concerns your posture. Sit up straight on your chair, lean forward, and bring your food to your mouth. Use a soupspoon or a tablespoon if available. Fill your spoon three quarters full and place the spoon in your mouth to eat. Do not slurp your soup. In American culture, it is rude to make any sound while eating, though in traditional Japanese and Chinese cultures, slurping is a compliment to the chef. If you want to get the soup from the bottom of the bowl, tilt the bowl away from you with one hand while scooping the soup into the spoon with the other hand away from you, lower the bowl to the table, and then lift the spoon and the contents to the mouth.

HINT: If the soup is too hot, gently blow into the bowl of soup. Avoid blowing on a spoon with soup in it because it is likely to spill and splatter. Another option is to scoop the soup portions closer to the bowl edge rather than on the center of the bowl. The outer portions are cooler, and the contents from the center of the bowl may burn your mouth.

Using your bread to soak up soup and then eat your bread is a no-no. Eat the bread separate from the soup. Crumbling your bread and sprinkling it on the soup is also a bad habit. Some casual establishments give crackers on the side for the soup. Placing these crackers into the soup is appropriate.

Onion Soup

Onion soup is delicious because of the cheese baked on top, but this also makes the soup tough to eat. The first step is to use your spoon or cheese knife to cut through the cheese. The cheese is often baked into the bowl, so it is dense on top and smoother below the surface. Use your spoon or cheese knife to cut the cheese from the bowl. Do not use your dinner knife. Scoop the soup from the bowl and cut away excess cheese from the spoon by pressing the spoon against the inside of the bowl. This process allows you to enjoy the soup without a soup trail or cheese strands from the bowl to your mouth.

Spaghetti and Other Long Pastas

You may like cutting your pasta into little easy-to-eat pieces, but this habit shows very poor table etiquette. Your pasta is served in a large pasta bowl with a large spoon. The spoon is about the size of a tablespoon or a little larger. Use your dinner fork to select a couple of the pasta strands with the tines and hold the tines against the bowl of the spoon. Turn the fork and pasta away from you until you have gathered the strands completely. Use the spoon bowl to keep the pasta in place so you can remove the food from the bowl and into your mouth without the contents falling down or strands falling loose. If a pasta strand falls loose, simply place the fork and paste against the spoon in the bowl and try to raise the fork to eat again. Do not eat with the spoon provided. The spoon is only there to assist you. Do not suck pasta into your mouth or take in so much pasta that you are using your lips and teeth to gather all the food. It does not only show poor character; no one wants to watch food hang from your mouth.

Oysters

Oysters are served many ways, but the two most common and complicated ways are oyster on a half shell and oysters Rockefeller. You can enjoy them both stress free and with ease.

Oyster on a Half Shell

Oyster on a half shell is a raw oyster with the top half of the shell removed. Most upscale restaurants present the shell on a platter covered in ice with condiments on the side. Normally, the condiments are horseradish, cocktail sauce, lemon wedge or lemon juice, and sometimes a vinaigrette sauce the chef creates. The platter is placed in the center of the table or passed around to each guest. Take one oyster with the shell and the condiments and place it on your plate. Use your fork to loosen the oyster from the shell and tilt the shell to remove any excess water. Put the condiments you would like and the lemon juice on the oyster.

You have two options for eating the oyster: (1) use your seafood fork to lift the oyster from the shell and put it into your mouth, or (2) pick up the oyster shell at the wider portion, which is toward the back. Tilt the shell slightly close to your mouth and allow the oyster to slide in. Some people swallow the oyster whole or gently bite down a couple of times and swallow. Do not rest the shell on your lip as you slide the oyster in your mouth because of the barnacle pieces that may end up on your lips.

Oysters Rockefeller

Oysters Rockefeller is an oyster on a half shell that have been backed or broiled with spinach, cheese, parsley, butter, and sometimes breaded. Leave the shell on the plate and use your fork to pick the oyster from the shell and enjoy.

Mussels

Mussels are eaten two ways: traditional and modern. Both are acceptable in upscale and casual settings, but traditional requires you to use your hands more, so avoid using the traditional technique if you are concerned about staining your clothes and having sauce on your fingers.

Traditional

For the traditional style, take a whole cooked mussel in your hand. Pull back the top part of the shell until it snaps off. Use the shell half to scrape the mussel meat from the shell and into your mouth. You only need to break one mussel in half and use the same shell half to remove the meat from all other mussels.

Modern

When using the modern technique, hold the mussel with your thumb and forefinger. Use your fork to gently twist the meat from the shell. The shell may be discarded in a separate bowl or pushed aside.

HINT: Do not eat the meat from closed shells. The open shells with exposed meat are the healthy mussels to eat. Before cooking, the chef discards open mussels because they are dead and unhealthy. After cooking, he or she also discards the shells that did not open because they are unsafe to eat as well.

Artichoke

Artichoke is very good and tasty for you. It is prepared either boiled or boiled and then broiled with seasoning with dipping sauce on the side. Artichoke is eaten with your hands. Pull off one leaf at a time and dip the soft center into the dipping sauce provided. Use your teeth to scrape the soft center from the leaf. Do not eat the entire leaf. Discard the remainder of the leaf by setting it on the side of your plate. When all the leaves are off, you are left with a soft stem and center. Use your fork and knife to cut the stem and eat.

Corn on the Cob

Needless to say, I would not recommend eating corn on the cob on the first date, but if you do find yourself at a picnic and corn on the cob is served, enjoy it. If you have a cob holder, stick the holder into each end of the cob. Rub a pat of butter on the corn. The best way to handle the butter is with a fork (tines hold the butter down toward the corn). Rotate the cob as you rub the pat of butter entirely over the corn on the cob. Use both hands to hold the corn and eat.

Another way to eat the corn is by cutting the kernels off the cob. Cutting kernels may seem a little prissy, but by doing so, the kernels do not get stuck between your teeth. Placing a cob holder on the end of the cob, take a steak knife and cut down the cob while holding up the cob at a diagonal. The kernels fall from the cob separately or in strips. Use your fork to eat the corn as if it was never on the cob. If you do choose to remove the corn with your teeth, remove kernels and particles from your teeth with your tongue, with your mouth closed, or excuse yourself to pick the food from your teeth in the restroom. Travel-size flossing tools are great to have in your handbag.

7

"Surround yourself with only people who are going to lift you higher." –Oprah Winfrey

The Host With The Most

My parents were never the social butterflies, jetting off to parties or hosting small or large gatherings at our house. A once-every-few-years BBQ with my grandparents and a couple of close friends was the extent of our Dawson family parties. When I was old enough to determine what kind of an adult I wanted to be, I knew throwing a party and having close friends over at least a couple of times a year was a must for me.

Knowing my personality, I only invited very close friends to my house but hosted larger events outside the house. I would create a theme for the night and reserve a space at a club or a restaurant: karaoke night, cowboy night at a local ranch-style club, or movie night. I only had two rules: don't break my budget (which was always little to nothing) and make sure my guests had fun. I walked away knowing I greeted each guest and hoped they had a good time.

Party Planning

Know Your Budget

The first step in organizing a party is deciding on a budget for your event. You don't want to spend three months' worth of salary to feed and entertain your friends. Plan a meal, entertainment, and decorations; use your income surplus. Price food and drinks by the plate, and work in entertainment and decorations after. Having a great band but quickly depleting food and drinks is not a good party. Also, decide whether you will rent a location to entertain your guests or hold the party at your home or in a location without an entrance fee. Make a realistic budget and stick to it. Plan and budget the meal first, and then the entertainment, the location, and the decorations.

Location, Location, Location

The location of your event is just as important as the food and the entertainment, and it includes the decorations. Choose a comfortable place for your party guests. You should have a seat for each person and tables for drinks. Your home is a wonderful location because you are familiar with the grounds, making it easier to decorate and manage the movement, and everything you need is at your fingertips. The most important consideration when choosing a party location is accessibility and the comfort of your guests. Your party should not burden your guests. They are there because they enjoy your company.

Night Club

All guests can enter with ease. You have a section or a VIP area reserved.

Restaurant

Reserve a private location so guests can move around comfortably.

You can request a preset menu.

Pool Hall, Bowling Alley

Reserve a portion of the location with the pool tables and lanes needed, depending on the size of your party.

Your Home

Choose a room in your home that people will feel most comfortable in. Make sure guests have easy access to a bathroom.

Plan Your Limits

How many guests can you entertain comfortably? After knowing your budget and the location, you must make your guest list. This can be the hardest part. If you can only entertain six people comfortably and safely, stick to six. You should also consider your entertainment experience. Unless you are planning a wedding or a social occasion, which traditionally requires a long guest list, make sure your event is at a size you can handle. Many guests want to see and talk to the host, so you don't want to host a party where no one has access to you because you are running around preparing food and hopping from one guest to another.

Theme

One of the best parts about hosting a party is planning a theme. You can entertain your friends with a rock band or in a haunted house. Summer pool party and Christmas party are the most common types of events. The only rule is to make your theme fun and relatable. Don't require your guests to step out of their comfort zones to have a great time. If you are going to have a pool party, don't require them to wear a bathing suit and get in the pool. If you have a guest who has a broken leg, don't hold a party that involves hike into the woods without providing assistance. Make your theme welcoming and comfortable for all guests.

Invitations

Invitations are the first sign of a good time that your guest will see.

Today, we have online invitations, and many of us use social networking sites to invite friends, but a mailed invitation goes a long way. You can create a personalized invitation, and your guests will know you spent a significant amount of your time creating your invitation and paid close attention to the complete presentation.

Online invitations are fantastic too if you put your work into creating a digital invite. I have received dancing e-mails, exploding gift e-invitations, and other exciting and impressive online invites. Online invitations are cost-effective and can be creative, but they can also give the impression of haste, laziness, and bad planning. Your guests will not be excited to set aside time to attend your event if you yourself don't show excitement about your party, starting with your invitations. They are going to play off your attitude from beginning to end.

Who's Who

The guests at your party should complement your night events and goals. Your list should also include old and new friends, returned invitations, "experts" who enjoy sharing and talking, and family members.

Party Planning Example

Theme: Movie night

Location: Your home

Goal for the night: Entertain friends, learn and enjoy a great film, allow your old friends to get to know your new friends

Guest list. Your close friend who wants to get into acting, a coworker you've grabbed drinks and a movie with, a close friend who is a movie critic writer, and the couple who always invites you over to their events

With the above guests, you can introduce your best friend to your coworkers, talk to the "open and talkative movie critic expert" about the movie, and return an invitation to the couple that wants to get to know you.

Vary your guests at each party so none of your friends feel exempt. The more often you entertain, the smaller your guest list becomes. One the other hand, entertaining once a year allows you to play host to a longer guest list since you would want to include all your friends.

Seating

Your table(s) should fit all your guests comfortably. Make sure your table has enough room for arms and legs for people to move, eat, and drink. If you have multiple tables, divide the guests into couples, singles, and common ground. Your table should have people with common interests, people with the same marital statuses, and introverts and extroverts. Before placing your guests, think of their interests and what type of dinner party you are hosting.

Questions

Is this a socializing-only event where everyone knows each other?

Is this a professional or work-related party?

Is any one of the guest single?

What are the common interests of the guests?

Seat each guest according to your knowledge of him or her.

If you have a guest of honor or a special guest, you should seat the honoree or the special guest next to the host; a female guest usually sits to the right of the host, while a male guest usually sits to the left of the hostess. You can also seat her or him at the other end of the table. If he or she has a date or a guest, seat that person by her or his side.

When you have a guest with special needs, cater to her or his needs, make him or her feel comfortable, and make sure she or he can access the restroom with ease.

As a host, you should sit at the head of the table. If you are co-hosting a party, one host should sit at each end of the table so both hosts can entertain each side of the table. If you are co-hosting a smaller dinner party (no more than five) and your co-host is your partner, it is acceptable for you to sit by his side while he sits at the head of the table.

HINT: Avoid sitting together people who are not fond of each other. Also, avoid sitting couples and best friends side by side. Seating arrangement should allow guests to get to know one another.

Write a table chart before the dinner party to help you match people accordingly; use placement cards on the table so guests know where they should sit. Your job as a host is to make sure people have a wonderful time at your party, so pay close attention to the seating arrangement. When the table conversation takes a lull, you should start a topic that more than one person would be interested in so everyone will be engaged and include himself or herself in the conversation.

Example: List of Guests with Connections
- Host has sports in common with Mr. Jones.
- Sally is an actor who is single, outgoing, and talkative.
- Michael is a single friend from work, is an introvert, but would love to try acting.
- Mr. Jones, a movie critic, loves sports.
- Mrs. Jones is a small flower shop owner.
- Mr. Peters, a close friend, is opening up a small business.
- Mrs. Peters enjoys old movies.

Cater to Your Guests' Needs
You should cater to your guests' needs. Greet everyone at the door when you can. Tour your guests around the major locations, like the restrooms, the dancing area, the bar, etc. Plan your music ahead of time with appropriate time and songs on your MP3 player or with the band. You don't want your guests to miss anything at your party, so point them in the direction where the fun and excitement is so you can continue to mingle and make sure everyone is having a great time. If you plan and direct every minute of your party, you will make sure the fun of the party never wanes and the guests never get bored. Make sure all the events move along at an appropriate time frame. Plan for the best, yet prepare for the unexpected by knowing the needs of each guest.

HINT: Mishaps happen, so be prepared. When planning an outside event, make sure you have a heating plan or an indoor option in case the weather turns cold or wet. If you are accident-prone with drinks, prepare a backup outfit.

Drinks and Food

Always prepare food that your guests can eat. If you have a guest who cannot eat a particular food because of allergies or religion, make a meal that all the guests can enjoy without them picking out certain items or avoiding a particular dish. If one or more of your guests are vegetarians or vegans, or they follow a lifestyle or beliefs with certain food restrictions, prepare a special meal for them. Ask them what food they like, or if they would like for you to get entrées from their favorite specialty eateries or markets.

When you are serving alcoholic beverages, you should give the option for nonalcoholic drinks.

Are You Being the Most . . . Dramatic?

Be on your best behavior no matter what. A drink being spilled on your dress, a guest of honor being late, or a guest arriving in a foul mood can throw you into a tizzy; but keep a smile and push yourself to have a great time. Small or major blunders don't have to ruin the night. Remember, your guests took some time off their schedules to spend some time with you. You should respect their time and be on your best behavior.

A Good Host Does Not...

- Drink too much
- Yell or throw fits at guests or the hired help
- Disappear for longer than five to ten minutes
- Complain or gossip to the guests
- Decide to not entertain or take part in the party
- Show any disdain with or toward a co-host
- Leave some guest left out

Fond Farewells

At the end of the night, it is very important to bid farewell to the guests

103

and thank them for coming. Try to remember one conversation topic you had so you can politely and quickly show them how important their conversation was to you.

Parting gifts are not required, but little bags of treats are wonderful at a special party, like a girls' night out or an honored guest dinner. Give simple tokens for the night, like chocolates and tea candles.

HINT: The end of this book has a checklist reminder for you as a dinner party guide so you always host a great dinner party.

8

"No one will take care of you if you don't take care of yourself." –Alicia Keys

Money Etiquette

Money management plays a major role in how we deal with everyday life, especially in sticky situations. Saving for a trip or saving for retirement is an everyday task, if not a monthly task, that requires careful planning and a disciplined attitude. Splurging on clothes, cars, or coffee and continually giving loans to friends can cause long-term problems for you. Mishandled funds can cause anxiety, end relationships, and limit your life experiences.

Limited experiences stunt your personal growth and social interactions. Many people believe etiquette and money go hand in hand as determining factors in having or not having enough money; therefore, having a lot of money automatically equals class and etiquette. Nothing can be farther from the truth. Money etiquette is being smart with your money and making sure your life is secure and has minimal debt by living within your means.

Earnings & Expenses

The first step in managing your money is knowing how much you earn and what your expenses are. You can calculate your net pay and then make a list of what you spend on every month. Be honest with yourself. Include your weekly trips to the coffee shop, entertainment with friends, and manicures. The easiest way to keep track is to keep your receipts and mark what you bought and why you bought them. Just a quick note works.

Putting a note on a receipt stops you from trashing it as extra paper in your purse, and it reminds you of what you spent your money on weeks prior. Keep all receipts in a file and calculate your total expenditures.

Another option is to use technology to keep track of your spending habits. Mint.com offers an excellent application online or on your mobile phone that records the amount of money you spend, categorizes what type of expenditure an item is (i.e., household bills, food, transportation, shopping, etc.), and keeps track of banking and credit card fees, loan payments, and the value of your properties (cars, homes, land, etc.). Mint.com also offers budgeting options, savings plans, and payment or fee alerts.

Regardless of whether you keep records of your expenditures on paper or through online resources, you must be honest and disciplined if you want to get your financial life in order.

Savings

Stashing away money for unexpected situations or for retirement can be tough when you see a beautiful dress in the window and gorgeous shoes to match with it. Saving does not have to mean you deprive yourself of the wonderful things and experiences you can have today. It means planning for your future.

If you make a plan and stick to it, you can work out how you can purchase a vacation package and wear the shoes and the dress on your trip. Sit down with a financial advisor, or budget out how much you can afford to put in a savings plan. Realistically, you should save three months' worth of living expenses if you do not own a house and eight months' worth of living expenses if you own a house and/or have a family.

Saving Options
Have a set amount of money automatically pulled from your paycheck or an account and placed in a savings account.

IRAs – Traditional or Roth (setting aside $125 in a Roth IRA will allow you to retire with over $300,000 at age sixty-five). Educate yourself on each type of IRA so you are aware of taxes and the amount you would like to have when you retire.

CD – Certificate of deposit is used as a savings account with a fixed interest rate and a fixed term for maturity at which you can withdraw your money.

MMA or MMDA – Money market accounts are a deposit account that you invest in the government and in corporate securities. Your interest rate is based on the current interest rate. The upside is you have the option to withdraw money from an MMA up to six times.

Stocks – Though stocks are not a great savings plan since the value of a share fluctuates, causing them to be a high-risk investment, they are helpful in investing a small portion of your money in a growing stock.

HINT: Arming yourself with knowledge about stocks, portfolios, and investing is a great asset. Many people are interested in company shares and stocks and are impressed when you can share your insight on the subject.

Do your research and learn about stocks, portfolio, and other similar subjects. You could be the hit of the party because you possess beauty and brains.

You should always have an emergency fund and a retirement fund. It may seem daunting at first, and you may want to buy clothes and handbags instead of investing; but if you think of the items that you have purchased and given away, or the money you drank away for a pricey latte, it will be a lot easier for you to cut back (not eliminate) on frivolous spending.

Spending Habits

Your spending habits influence how you view your life. If you spend money by charging up your credit cards, but you cannot pay your bills, you may have some money management problems. If you loan money to friends but never get paid, you may want to find some new friends or address the problem soon. Buying numerous frivolous items that lose their value will always cause a shortage of funds that you could have invested in greater assets or better experiences, such as a house, a designer handbag, or a vacation. Keep track of your spending style and see where you are mishandling your money, and make a change. Below are a few uncomfortable money situations and some wise choices.

Loans

Your friend has asked you for a loan. We have all heard that money and friends do not mix. The truth is, either money and friends can make friendships stronger, or money can tear friendships apart. If a friend needs financial help and you can provide it, by all means, help him or her; but attach a document detailing how he or she will pay you. I only write up a contract when the money is big and I need it returned. Avoid contracts for loans of $20 or less. You'll just look like a jerk. The other option is to give your friend the money as a gift. Giving the money as a gift (no strings attached) makes you feel good helping a friend in need and eases the tension caused by worrying when you will get paid. Accompany the gift with a very clear and stern statement that he or she cannot ask money from you again. This will give her or him what he or she needs and keep the friendship healthy, and you will never have to worry about financing your friend's financial emergencies.

If you lent money and it's past the date you thought you should get paid, or you see your friend wearing fabulous new shoes, don't demand payment by attacking her. Privately and politely ask your friend when she will return your money. Be kind. The shoes could be a gift, or her paycheck may be clearing her account the next day. Always be polite and ask for definite dates and plans for the payment.

My mother always said, "Never lend money you cannot afford to lose." If your friend does not have the means or has no intentions of returning your money, let it go as a lesson learned. If it is a large loan, you can always consider settling it in court and contact the IRS about including the loss in your taxes.

Never get a loan or an account in your name for a friend or a boyfriend. This includes cell phones, cars, homes, computers, cosigning, etc. If your friend needs your financial history and needs help to get these items, it means creditors see him or her as an unreliable consumer, and you should see her or him the same way. It's one thing to be understanding and helpful, but if you help your friend with a loan your credit history will be affected by his or her actions and financial situations. Offer financial advice, such as a debt counselor who worked for you or a friend in the past. Politely tell the person, "No. I don't like to get involved in financial obligations with friends."

You Owe Money, but You're in a Financial bind

This is a very sticky situation and an uncomfortable position to be in, either as the lender or as the borrower. You should never borrow money that you cannot return. It is better to ask for small monetary gifts from several people than ask one large loan from one person. If you owe someone money, acknowledge your financial obligation. Make plans to pay. If you can only afford $20 every week to pay an $80 loan, let the lender know about it when you borrow the money. Put your agreement in writing. The person will feel confident and secure that he or she will get her or his money back.

Men and Romantic Partners Borrowing Money

I have a rule for myself when it comes to men and money. If a man that I am dating borrows money from me, I'll run for the hills. I am excluding running to the grocery store, loaning $20 dollars or so during outings, etc. Give the money.

Many men pay for dates and most outings. I willingly give money or pay for grocery store runs for events. When a man asks to borrow a large sum of money, I raise my eyebrows . . . even if he pays it back. I question the financial responsibility of the man I am dating. Many of us date to meet a partner we can grow with emotionally and financially. If he is borrowing money from you, he may be doing it often with many of his friends, and it could be a sign of a bigger problem. Money loans and romance do not mix.

"Fuck You" Money

What is, Fuck You Money? FYM is something every woman should have. When you are ready to walk away from a relationship or a marriage you must have enough money to support you and any children you may have. Keep an account with only your name on it. It does not have to be a secret from your other half unless you choose to do so. But, you must have enough money for a moving truck, an apartment, food, and anything else you need to survive without the person you plan to leave. "Fuck you" money is so you can say, "Fuck you! Fuck this! I'm leaving!"

Backing Out of a Financial Obligation

Many of us plan a vacation with our girlfriends or offer to pay for a large gift with the intention of paying our share. But sometimes life happens, and we find ourselves in a financial bind when it is time to pay.

The first thing to do is to tell the parties involved that you cannot afford to pay your share. Let them know you are forfeiting your slot or payment in hopes of getting back on financial track. Offer the amount you can pay if other people lose money because of your financial problems.

Vacations

If it is a vacation, your friends may have to entirely cancel the vacation without your share, so offer to pay the cancellation fee if you can. It's better to pay a small fee than go on a vacation you cannot afford. Your friends will be bummed out they missed a vacation, but they will be happy they did not lose money because of you. You can also find another friend who may want to go in your stead. This way, you save money and make everyone happy.

Group Gifts

If you offered to chip in for a gift and found out that you could not afford your share at the last minute, inform your friends of your financial strain. Offer what you can afford and/or offer to pick up the gift or run errands in relation to getting the gift.

Tips for Group Gifts Savings

Stashing away money for unexpected situations or for retirement can be tough when you see a beautiful dress in the window and gorgeous shoes to match with it. Saving does not have to mean you deprive yourself of the wonderful things and experiences you can have today. It means planning for your future.

- Be honest with yourself and with all parties involved about what you can afford.
- Always suggest a gift within your budget.
- If you cannot afford everyone's budget, plan to get your own gift or offer to do cost-free errands related to the gift (picking up, wrapping, delivering, etc.).

Charitable Giving

It is always great to give your time and your money to charities that are dear to you and the people close to you. Giving to a charity is not a requirement, but a positive gesture to show someone or a group you believe in their cause. Helping local and national charities also increases our knowledge about the woes in the world and shows our empathy to those who are less fortunate. Give, give, and give what you can afford to give. Keep in mind that a person should only ask you once or twice every year to give to their charities.

Family

Family members come around several times a year to ask for money, so plan on a set amount that you feel comfortable giving. If you have a lot of children in your family who ask for fund-raising, let their parents know you have set aside an amount for each charity. This allows you to not be overwhelmed by saying yes or no and ensures that one child does not get more than the other child gets. If you cannot afford to give to every charity in small amounts, ask your family members to tell you which one means the most to them, and give to that particular charity.

Friends

Decide which charities mean the most to you and give to them. If a friend asks for your help for Save the Star Fund and you are not interested in saving any stars, let him or her know you have already selected your charities and budgeted out for your giving.

You're Asking

Like your friends and family, you should only ask once or twice a year for charitable giving to a charity that is close to your heart. If you are giving to their charities, they should give to yours. You can also keep track of which charities people give to you for the future. Keeping a record of people's giving can serve you in many ways: You can send a thank-you card, with the outcome of their donation and updated information on the charity. You will know which charities your friends and family give, so you can have a more targeted list of who gives to which of your charities. You can also keep track of how often you ask for charities and how often each person gives, so if you've asked twice without receiving, you know to not ask anymore.

Stay Frugal and Fabulous

Frivolous spending happens. We will always want a new pair of shoes, a three-dollar cup of coffee, or cuter little outfits for our pets. When you control how much and how often you spend your money on these items, you are managing your finances well. If you want to spend more money on your "wants" but don't have the budget to do so, you can create ways to accumulate more money.

Make more $$$

Are you good at something? You can get a part-time job or work from home doing something you are good at. Can you knit, edit photos, or bake cupcakes? Find a special skill you can do that people will pay you for your services. You can also take a class to learn a trade, such as fitness training, a nail technician course, or sewing. A little bit of your extra time can earn you a lot of money to buy those new shoes and a designer handbag to match.

Do not do free work for friends, family, or anyone else. Your time and skills are valuable. Make an equal trade for service; request a gift card of your favorite store or a meal if you don't want to demand cash. Give your friends the same courtesy when they provide you with a service you would normally pay for.

Create a Blog or a Website

When you create a vlog (video blog) or a blog about something you have knowledge on or something related to your career, you create a consultancy career and a continued following and need for your advice and knowledge. As a result, you become an expert in your line of work. If you work in a nine-to-five job as a human resources representative, you can create a blog about the pitfalls of an unprepared interviewee or an advice website for hiring managers.

You do not have to be a CEO of a company or a *New York Times*–praised expert. You simply have to know your product and what you are offering. Chances are, if you are an administrative assistant, you can vlog about the best ways to file or consult for a small-business owner about administrative skills so they can survive without full-time administrative help. By creating an online site, you can attract attention to your skill, making your advice valuable and solidifying your reputation as an expert in your field.

Save Money on Your Everyday Needs

Start using coupons and online saving websites. You should try to save at least 50 percent on everything that you need in life. Many websites and applications cater to the frugal-minded, helping you put your money on savings or on your other special purchases. Bookmark and download price-comparison websites and/or sites that have promotional codes to save on your everyday needs, like grocery shopping, dry cleaning, or that latte you can't live without.

HINT: New discount websites and promotions are online and are available as an application almost every day, so do a search on your computer and phone at least once a month.

Also, ask stores you frequent for the websites they advertise their sales and promotions on.

Money Matters and Sticky Situations

A friend asks how much you spent on your house, an expensive coat, etc., and you don't want to share

I would rather not think about the price. I need to focus on decorating or working the coat in my wardrobe.

You paid for a group gift and have not been reimbursed by the rest of the group.

Send a group e-mail informing everyone the gift has been purchased and telling them when you would like the money. If a couple of friends in the group have not paid, contact them directly.

A friend always complains about not having money or having a financial strain.

Politely confront her about her complaining. She may not know her bad habit. Don't lend money, but offer an ear and suggest solutions, like a financial advisor. Don't get too involved. Suggest and move on.

You bought a fake and someone thinks it's real and asks about it.

You can buy a fake version of any item today and pass it off as the real thing. Don't fret and don't lie. You can choose to be honest or tell them you love your item and why. It's no one's business but yours.

Your friends plan events that are above your budget.

Start planning events that fit your budget. Look for free or low-cost fun events that you and your friends would enjoy.

You bought an item from the local thrift or consignment store but are too embarrassed to tell your friend the truth.

You have nothing to be embarrassed about. A great find is something to celebrate about. If you choose to keep your frugal finds private, you can tell them stores that carry the same type of item. You can also say you bought it a while ago. "This old item? Thanks for liking it."

9

"Love is easy! Kindness is easy. So I try to acknowledge everyone that reaches out to me. I can't control the rest of Twitter- but I try to make my page a safe place for people." –Yvette Nicole Brown

Technology Etiquette

Cell phones, Internet, social networking, and other types of technology have grown to a degree where society depends on them daily. We use social networks to stay acquainted with our loved ones, share photos and video of events in our lives, and simply find information about anything and everything. Though we use modern technology to keep in touch with society, these devices can also be used to destroy our lives and the people we love. Having technology etiquette will keep you safe as well as keep your private life private.

Cell Phones

It seems that everyone has a cell phone. From young children to the elderly, everyone is using a cell phone to call family and friends, check e-mail, map directions, or find the best restaurant in town. Your cell phone could be the most important device you own, but it can also be an annoyance to other people if you are not mindful. Know when your phone can be a disturbance, and make proper adjustments so other people wouldn't want to throw you and your phone out the door.

Turn Cell Phones Off or Switch to Silent Mode
Weddings and funerals (even vibration can disturb a ceremony)
Movies, plays, recitals, church
Job interviews
Tests or exams

Put Your Phone on Vibrate Mode
Dinner with friends
Dates
Casual meetings
Work or class
Libraries
Public transportations

On certain locations and during certain events, it is disturbing to hear a phone ring, but it is irksome to make a phone call or text. If you must make a phone call or send a text, excuse yourself and walk away to a private area and place the call or send the text discreetly. Many friends understand if you must send a text during casual outings, but do so sparingly and quickly and don't make it a habit.

Cell Phone Bad Behavior
Talking about personal business in public.

Gossiping about people in public. You should not gossip, and doing it using a cell phone in public shows poor character, and you could be in the presence of an acquaintance of the person you are talking about and not know it.

Texting long messages. Keep them simple and short.

Do not send a text full of texting codes or emoticons, such as LOL,

IDK, ;-p, etc. Many people do not know what they stand for.

If you know that a person is driving, don't text him or her. Assuming she or he has a hands-free device, it is safer for him or her to talk to you rather than read and respond to a text.

Talking aloud. Keep your voice down. People don't want to hear your conversation.

Calling and texting while driving. Use a hands-free device.

When riding on a bus or a train, keep your voice down and conversations short. Many people commute to work, read, or simply use their commuting time to relax. They don't want to hear about your new outfit for the party.

If someone calls you, call her/him back. Do not text back unless your response is "In the middle of _____, I'll call you back in 20." It is rude to text back when a person took the time to call you.

Do not send a provocative, potentially embarrassing, or confidential text. This information can easily be shared intentionally or accidentally.

When sending a text to a person for the first time, include your name and introduce yourself. For example, "Hello, this is Jane from class . . ."

Do not give bad news through text or over the phone. Sometimes a phone call is our only option, but a text is in very poor taste and bad judgment when relating bad news and painful information.

Be patient when waiting for phone calls and text messages. In today's world, people are always on the go, so don't get upset if you do not get a response immediately.

If you send two text messages without a response, do not send another. The person is either busy or not interested.

You have control over your cell phone and your life, so make it important for you to return text within twenty-four hours and phone calls within forty-eight hours.

Gyms, Locker Rooms, Dressing Rooms, Restrooms, Spas

Your phone should never be answered or used in any place where people assume complete privacy. In locker rooms and dressing rooms, people change clothes and are nude around other people they may or may not know. A person is assuming privacy in these facilities and respect from the people that use them. A person with a cell phone out in a private place can make everyone feel uncomfortable. If you must answer the phone, walk to a private location where you are alone.

The public areas of a gym and spas are common places where cell phones are used because of the multiple uses these gadgets offer. Gyms and spas are designed for people who want to focus on self-improvement and relax, and when a person is talking loudly on the phone, he or she disturbs everyone within earshot. Keeping your voice down and your conversation short will show others your good manners and respect for your fellow gym and spa members.

Recording Video and Taking Pictures

Many cell phones have cameras, voice recorders, and video recorders to capture our life experiences. Knowing these devices are always around us, and being aware of our behavior and actions, are more important today than twenty years ago. Your next outburst or topless karaoke performance can be online or e-mailed to hundreds of people before you realize what happened. These images of you can surface anywhere and can be seen by anyone, when you least expect it. Once information is placed online or on someone's phone, it takes on a life of its own, and there is rarely anything we can do to stop it before the world sees it.

The best way to avoid this pitfall is to think before you act. In modern society, you must ask yourself, *if my parents, loved ones, or boss saw this information or action, would I be proud of it?* If you say no, don't do it. Many years ago, we could make a mistake and move on, but with technology surrounding us, one little mishap could follow us for the rest of our lives.

We see many celebrities taking naked pictures of themselves and tweeting or sharing questionable behavior online, but these people have hired publicists, managers, and other staff to make sure they can correct bad choices. Majority of us do not have this luxury, so we will have to manage our lives on our own.

Things to Avoid Doing in Front of a Cell Phone Recorder

Yelling at anyone in public (in coffee shops, in stores, at a law enforcer, at ex-friends, etc.). Handle your grievances face-to-face and calmly.

Dancing on a stripper pole if you are not at a private party or a pole dancing class.

Pole dancing has become a popular exercise as well as a girls'-night-out fun. If images are recorded, they can be easily misconstrued. Make it your business to not record friends and have friends not record you, unless you are a professional pole dancer and displaying your skill level is part of your job.

Performing a striptease for anyone outside your bedroom.

Taking pictures of your private parts or near-naked body, and then texting or e-mailing them to anyone. Don't even send to your lover photos of yourself scantily clad. Instead, send him a short text or slip scented notes in his pocket, like, "I've got a surprise for you when you get home." Notes give mystery and keep your dignity intact.

Getting into physical altercations.

Taking pictures of or recording yourself and your love interest making out or kissing.

Stealing, lying, sticking up your middle finger, and spitting are all bad behaviors and should not be done at all, and definitely not in front of a camera.

Doing bathroom activities.

Social Networks

Social networks have been a popular way to keep in touch with friends and family. We can also meet like-minded people and share our hobbies, interests, and professional skills with many people from all over the world. With the expanding use of social networks, our private lives have become less private. If or when you choose to create a social network account, your private life can remain private because you have complete control of your page, assuming it does not get hacked or copied.

When creating a social network account ask yourself, *why am I creating the social page?* Do you want to keep in touch with friends and family, reconnect with an old love, date, or network and join social events?

Having an idea of what you want your page used for helps you determine what type of information you should share when you post comments, pictures, information, etc. You can always create more than one account, keeping one page for your private life with close friends and family and another page for networking with coworkers or professional use. The most important step to take is setting up your privacy settings so you feel comfortable with the information you share. Though you can block people, erase friends, or control the contents other people see, know that this is not 100 percent foolproof.

Remember, anything that is online can be hacked or copied. If you use your page for personal use, accept only those people you are close to and trust. Your networking page can be viewed by coworkers and networking associates, so write only work-related or inspirational information on the page. Do not post negative information: "I hate my job," or "Suzanne in printing needs help." These types of information are a red flag to your current employer and a potential new employer. If you prefer to have one account only and accept your family, close friends, and those "friends" whom you know professionally on the same account, be very careful.

Do not post private life events and private photos, and most important, monitor what other people post, especially photos of you that they upload. Inform the people you allow to access your page that your social network page is for both professional and private uses. If people post information that you do not approve of, let them know and politely ask them to stop.

Example: "Jane, can you please remove on your page that picture of me dancing? I really don't want this picture to be on the web. Thank you."

A friend will understand, and he or she should remove it. If she or he continues to post unacceptable information or compromising pictures of you, the only action you can do to protect yourself is to delete the person from your account.

Removing a friend from your social network account does not mean deleting him or her from your life. There are people whom you may not feel comfortable bringing into your professional life.

Do not make it a personal attack. Also, removing a person from your account will not stop her or him from posting information about you. A deleted person or a "non-friend" cannot post on your wall, so you and your friends will not be bothered by any information from him or her. Politely inform her or him of your choice to keep your personal life and professional life separate.

A friend will understand, and he or she should remove it. If she or he continues to post unacceptable information or compromising pictures of you, the only action you can do to protect yourself is to delete the person from your account. Removing a friend from your social network account does not mean deleting him or her from your life. There are people whom you may not feel comfortable bringing into your professional life. Do not make it a personal attack. Also, removing a person from your account will not stop her or him from posting information about you. A deleted person or a "non-friend" cannot post on your wall, so you and your friends will not be bothered by any information from him or her. Politely inform her or him of your choice to keep your personal life and professional life separate.

Negative Post

It has become more common for people to share their frustrations with their employers and ex-loves, their day-to-day whereabouts, whom they are in a relationship with, and why a relationship ended. Your close friends and family members do want to know if you have a broken heart or if you had to work a fourteen-hour shift and has little sleep, but you should avoid posting this information on the web.

Your moment of frustration or emotional bliss can turn into a lifetime of giving explanations. If you post, "You are slime, Joe. I wish I never met you," you may get the sympathy you want, but you could lose the trust of a friend, stop potential good mates from wanting to get to know you, and experience many other negative outcomes. Your intention might be to offend the one who hurt you, but negative posts hurt your reputation and impair good judgment, causing people to steer clear of you because they might be next on your negative post list.

Live by this rule: "Say it, forget it. Write it, regret it!" If you tell a person to her or his face how you feel, you two can discuss the issue and move on. If you post, text, or e-mail negative information, it will come back to haunt you.

HINT: If you don't want the world to know certain information or see a certain picture, don't post it. Use the same regard and caution when you post information about other people.

The Unwanted

Just like in the real world, people choose to do cruel and mean-spirited actions on the web. Internet users gossip, threaten, and do a lot of things to destroy your character on the net. Unfortunately, this behavior is common regardless of whether the person who is trying to destroy you knows you or not. One way to stop being harassed or bullied online is to contact the website owner and ask him or her to remove the unpleasant information. Continue reporting the negative information. If the bullying happens on a social network, you can block the user and report the person to the website company. With persistence, the website will eventually erase the information and/or block the bully. Another option is to contact the bully and ask him or her to stop. If the offender is anonymous, it will be harder to get her or his contact information. You can contact the website owner for the IP address of the user, but many sites do not give out this information without a request from law enforcement or an attorney, so save all the information you can find on the net.

In some cases, ignoring the person and his or her posts is the best option. People will get bored and move on. If you are a private citizen, reporting and ignoring might work. If the harassment continues, contact the police or an attorney to learn about your best options to protect yourself.

E-mails

I cannot live without logging on to my e-mail account every twenty minutes or so. People often e-mail information instead of calling. The following are a few ways to mind your manners.

Sending E-mails

Always include a subject line. Give the recipient the option to know what the topic is. On a busy day, an e-mail without a subject line can be easily missed.

When sending an e-mail to multiple recipients, use the bcc (blind carbon copy) to protect everyone's e-mail address. This option also makes the e-mail easier to read since the reader does not have to scroll down the page to get to the body of the message.

Before sending your e-mail, read it thoroughly and check for misspellings, omissions, and correct salutation.

Keep your language clean and positive in e-mails. E-mails can be shared and easily misinterpreted.

Do not use your work e-mail as your personal e-mail. Companies monitor Internet use and the contents of e-mails. Keep all e-mails professional while at work.

Forwards

Many people want to pass on religious, funny, sexual, charity, and chain e-mails. Don't pass these forwarded messages along unless you know it's okay for the recipients to receive these e-mails. Don't send them to their company e-mail addresses. Sexual and pornographic e-mails can get the recipients reprimanded.

Responding to E-mails

Respond to all e-mails as soon as possible. If you check your e-mail once a week or you have a few e-mail addresses, let people know how often you check your e-mail and how to get a quick response. They will appreciate knowing your e-mail habits rather than waiting for a response they are not going to get. Don't forget to let people know when you change your e-mail address or change jobs so they do not continue sending information you cannot receive.

Contact List and Information

Create a group contact list. Keeping an organized list of contacts in special groups makes sending e-mails easier and faster. Separate each person by relationships and privacy. I have my fellow cheerleaders on one list and my sisters on another list, so I never confuse the type of information each group will receive from me.

Photos Online

Sharing photos of our lives online is how we share our excitement and fabulous experiences. Many of us don't even print out photos anymore. Uploading photos and e-mailing them to family and friends or sharing them within an online community is common today. The social network and cell phone rules apply to sharing photos as well. Do not upload photos that you do not want your parents or grandparents to see. Photos of you behaving badly, doing compromising positions, having a bad day, or not looking good should not be posted on the net. Once uploaded, a picture can travel around and take on a life of its own. Show the same respect for current and ex-friends. Do not upload photos of people that show them in a negative or unflattering light.

Online Videos

The rules on sharing your photos apply to sharing videos as well. Video cameras can now record our everyday lives and the lives of people we know and do not know. YouTube and similar sites allow Internet users to watch the lives of people, whether they are enjoying music or dancing, doing their online shows, or are vlogging. If you are recording your performance or work, be professional. This video could be your calling card to get your career off the ground. It could also serve as a caution to producers, directors, or investors. Most people do not do business with a novice but take their chances with a professional.

An emergency takes place before your eyes. If you see an emergency in action, call 911 instead of only recording. Lend a hand when possible. It is your choice to be a part of the solution rather than just be a bystander.

Many times, videos help solve a crime or save a life. Always use caution when recording unsafe events. Safety first!

10

"Challenges make you discover things about yourself that you never really knew." –Cicely Tyson

The Art of Falling and Getting Up

I go to auditions almost every day of the week. Some auditions result in a person liking me and my work and hiring me, but many of them end in rejection. Dealing with rejection is tough. Many people take rejection as a failure or a fall from grace. But true strength and beauty is revealed during the hardest times. In my case, one of the hardest moments I struggled with was during the first few days after I left *The Price Is Right*.

I received a call from a producer one morning, informing me I was no longer needed in the show. I had just purchased my first home and was planning a future with the show. Needless to say, I was blindsided by the news, and what was even more hurtful was that many people knew of my departure before I did, and strangers on the Internet wanted to share their views—good, bad, and ugly. I was angry! I wanted to cry and voice out how hurt I was. I wanted to pound on doors and share how angry I was. Even with the pain in my heart, I realized that my three years with the production were some of my best days. I had to accept I had been a part of a historic show. I had a job many models and actresses would have loved to have . . . even for just a day. Many performers who are in the same position that I was in become angry and react wanting to inflict the pain they are feeling in others.

I chose to do what I do best. I thanked God for the experience. I sent a thank-you letter to the production and crew for the three years of great experience. Believe me, I was hurt, angry, and felt betrayed. I had never been let go from any job. But I knew I had worked hard and given my best every day. I wanted to walk away with my head held high and not feel shame or expect pity.

I am a better person now because of it. I had lived through a public fall and disappointment, but I had chosen to walk away with grace. I was confident in my past efforts and more prepared for my future.

Everyone should strive to be the best that he or she can be, but mistakes happen. You could lose your job, forget to introduce your date at a party, fail to respond to an RSVP, or rub the tummy of a person who is not pregnant. Minor and major faux pas are a part of life because life is not perfect, even if you strive to be perfect. Accept the missteps in life, but don't crumble through your journey or forget to learn from your experience. Grow from the situation and move on. The entire process of falling, brushing yourself off, and walking tall with grace and confidence is an art. The following are solutions to those inevitable blunders and fall from grace:

You Fail to Introduce People

Introducing someone is Etiquette 101, but sometimes you are pulled away unexpectedly, or you forget a person's name. Don't fret and don't avoid the introduction. If you can stop being pulled away, do so. Tell the people around you that you want to introduce someone. Follow the introduction etiquette, and then excuse yourself if you must go. Be sure to mention some commonalities so people can carry on with their conversation without you.

You Forget a Person's Name

There are two ways to handle name forgetfulness. If you have run through every part of your memory and cannot recall the name of the person standing in front of you, simply apologize and ask him or her for her or his name. Admit your blunder. Many people make jokes, attributing the mishap to old age or a crazy home life. If you remember meeting him or her in the past, mention at what event you were both present and inform her or him that it is great to see him or her again but that you cannot remember her or his name. Your other option is to introduce the person you know, and then hear the other person's name as he introduces himself of herself. The introduction should jog your memory enough to recall your last encounter.

You forgot to RSVP or Just Not Sure You'll Attend

This is a bad habit and limits the accommodations the host can provide for you. If it is a dinner party, the host may not have enough food or seats to accommodate the people who did not RSVP. Upon arrival, immediately apologize to the host.

Do not make a big production about your lack of consideration. Accept what the host can offer with a smile, whether it is a seat at the corner of the table or a couch to sleep on. Remember, the host is trying to make you feel welcome when you failed to acknowledge her or his time, money, and home.

In the future, always remember to RSVP and inform a host that you are arriving, and/or update him or her of your travel plans. Include your arrival and departure dates and times.

You Forget to Turn Off Your Phone or Put it on Vibrate Mode

Immediately turn off your phone. We all know the ringing tones of our mobile phones, so if your ringing tone starts with a silent ring, try to turn off your phone at that moment. If you must take the call, switch your tone to vibrate mode, excuse yourself, and take the call, away from everyone you might disturb. Remember to apologize when you return to them.

You Ignore Request and Accommodations from Your Host

Many invites come with a request: no children, monetary gifts only, outside barbecue, etc. Respect the wishes of the host. Do not bring children or gifts if he or she requests that you don't. Hire a babysitter. The host normally remembers who followed the rules and who did not, so be prepared to receive fewer invites to his/her events. If you did not realize that children are not invited and you brought your children, keep them by your side and pay close attention to them. You don't want them running around and interfering in the event.

If you want to bring a gift, mail it to the home of the host before the event. Many couples live together before they get married or have lived separately, so they don't need the traditional wedding gifts; therefore, they ask for monetary gifts.

If a party is to be held outside, you must prepare yourself for the environment. Your host should not be required to keep you warm or cool.

I Cannot Eat This, This, and Definitely not That!

Don't request your host to follow your diet unless you have severe allergies of certain foods and/or observe food restrictions prescribed by your religion. When you respond to an invitation, inform the host what your allergies or your religious requirements are and what you cannot eat. If you are simply on a diet or don't like green vegetable, don't bother the host with this information. At a dinner party, eat around the food you cannot eat. You should never go to a party famished, so such light eating should not affect you.

Gossip and Unwelcome Comments

Sometimes we share a comment that is in poor taste and hurtful. I have let words fall from my mouth that I soon regretted. Get in the habit of practicing what our mothers say: "If you don't have anything nice to say, don't say anything at all." Deciding not to say anything hurtful or not to make any comments that can be taken wrongly is good practice. If you said something that you wish you could take back, acknowledge your blunder, apologize, and move on.

If a gossip that you started gets around, go to the person at the heart of the gossip, admit your lack of candor, and apologize. Admitting your fault reminds you not to engage in ugly behavior and may save your friendship and your image. Talking behind a person's back can be seen as a cowardly and weak act. If you have a problem with a person, address him or her and the issue directly.

Apologies go a long way, so if you put your foot in your mouth, apologize. Do not disregard another person's disdain at your comment.

Acknowledge her or his pain and move on. You might have commented on a friend's weight, and the weight gain was a result of an illness. You gave hurtful words about a person's disheveled home, and he or she had just lost his or her job. Be aware of your thoughtless comments. There is always an explanation for a setback in a person's life. If you are concerned, meet with the person privately and express your concern.

Arguing in Public

Having a disagreement with anyone is uncomfortable, but turning the argument into a soap opera for all to see is worse. If you find yourself in a loud confrontation, it is best to calmly ask a person to lower her or his voice and discuss the situation in private.

If your request is ignored, kindly tell the person that the issue is important to you but that you will have to address the matter some other time, and then exit. Do not stay and perform the reality show drama or add fuel to the fire. Excuse yourself politely and address the problem when you are in a private place.

If the blowup has already caused a scene, apologize. Find the host and apologize for your behavior. You have no reason to discuss the outburst or explain away the saga. Let the host enjoy the party and send a card or an apology the following day.

Never start an argument with anyone in public. If a serious discussion arises, politely tell the person you would prefer to address the matter in private so you can give it the attention it needs.

You're Late

Being late is a sure way to let a person know you think very little of him or her. This may or may not be true, but the person will wonder why it is not important for you to be on time. Traffic, accidents, and flat tires happen. When they do, call the person and tell her or him that you are running late. He or she should understand if this is out of your character. If your tardiness is chronic, break that habit, lest people will see you as unreliable. This behavior could cost you your job or your relationship.

The Dreaded Check

A few scenarios can make the waiter placing the check on the table a dreaded situation. Planning can ease the pain of paying the tab. If your consumption is more than the other guests', you should always pay for your extra food and drinks. No one should pay for your five drinks when they only had one.

If you host a party at a restaurant, you should pay for the event. If you cannot afford to cover the cost, contact all the people who would attend the party and express your interest in having a gathering in honor of your friend. This way, everyone takes the responsibility of paying for himself or herself and the guest of honor. Your other option is to host a small gathering at your house or at an affordable place where you are comfortable picking up the tab.

If your portion of the bill is greater than your dates, offer to pay or offer to pay the tip. If your date shows dismay over the check and the consumed amount is evenly divided, offer to pay your part and seriously rethink if you are going out on a date with this person again. A gentleman will never complain about spending money or time with a person as wonderful as you.

If you plan to pay but your card is declined, immediately offer another form of payment. If you do not have another payment option, offer to go to the closest ATM or ask the manager what you can do to rectify the situation. Ask a friend to cover your share, but return his or her money immediately. You should always know your credit limit or your account balance.

Compromising Photos, Sex Tapes, and Nudies

Naked photos and sex tapes of new socialites seem to appear every other month. A nude photo, a sex tape, or a questionable picture can destroy your life. Don't get into the habit of videotaping your rendezvous or your private escapades with your lover or friends.

If such images are released online, contact the website owner to have them removed. If you e-mail videos accidentally, send an immediate apology and ask the recipient to trash the contents of the e-mail. You will quickly see who your friends are by the outcome of this situation.

Many foes release these images for personal gain. As unfortunate and uncontrolled this situation is and may become, it is best to write a letter requesting that the person responsible for the spread of the materials stop releasing them. The next step is to contact an attorney and/or your local police department. The authorities will be able to assist you and determine if any unlawful act has been done.

Whoever is with you in the images deserves an apology if you are responsible for releasing the material, whether it was intentional or accidental. Your life and his or her life will be affected, and acknowledgment must be made and an apology is due.

Your Private Life is Revealed to the Public

Private information you would prefer to keep to yourself sometimes comes out. As embarrassing as this may be, you can find strength in this unfortunate event. If the information comes from a person whom you entrusted it with, allow yourself some time to gain perspective. Don't approach him or her in anger. Tell him or her how you feel. Inform her or him you thought you could trust him or her. Express your pain and tell her or him how you would like him or her to handle your private information in the future, but never share your personal life with her or him again. You don't want to have a repeat offense.

We misjudge people sometimes, but don't make your misjudgment a habit. If you consistently trust mendacious people, look within yourself and take time to correct your bad habit of trusting people who do not have your best interest in mind.

You're not Miss Popularity

Throughout our lives, we make mistakes. We hurt people both intentionally and accidentally. That is life. Life has lessons that we have to learn the hard way, and people will not like us for it. The best way to win friends is to admit your wrongdoings and your shortcomings. People accept each other and relate to one another based on common characteristics. One characteristic that all humans have is that we are flawed and we make mistakes. An apology goes a long way. Apologize and express your reasons and feelings. Allow a person to digest the information and deal with her or his feelings by giving him or her the space he or she needs. Sending flowers, candy, or a card shows that you are thinking of her or him.

If the situation is not too detrimental to him or her, she or he will contact you in the future to rekindle your friendship. If he or she chooses to keep you on the unpopular list and never shares a friendship or a relationship with you again, take comfort in your efforts and learn your lesson from the experience.

You are Caught in a Lie

When you are caught in a lie or an exaggeration of the truth, admit it. Apologize if it requires one and move on.

You Talk About Yourself Too Much

Nerves can take over our brains and cause us to talk too much or not talk enough. If you are the type of person who clams up on first dates or in crowds, the only solution is to force yourself to talk more. Join public speaking clubs in your community and practice speaking. If you are the type of person who talks too much, on the other hand, ask people about themselves. People enjoy talking about themselves and love when a person is interested in their lives and love hearing their names said.

Talking too much about yourself without any regard for other people can come across as arrogance. To help break this habit, always ask follow-up questions to a person's story or ask him or her if anything in her or his life relates to what you just said. Monitor your talking time. If you talked for over three minutes straight, shut up! Let the other person in on the conversation.

Example: Jane: "So then I ordered every chocolate item the store had. Do you like chocolate?"

This technique allows the listener to take part in the conversation, which becomes a give-and-take between two people.

You Bash Your Employer and They Find Out

Never talk poorly about your employer online, on social networks, or through your office e-mail messenger. If such ill information is relayed to your employer or your boss, it could have detrimental effects on your employment or promotions.

Many people feel that your social network and e-mail behavior should be private or just between you and your "friends" on your private account. But the reality is, information gets around and bad news travels fast. If you want to express your disgust with your superior or your employer, talk about it privately at home. Use your e-mail at home to write to friends and complain about work. The Internet is a public bulletin board. Do not write negative information about anyone or anything that you don't want your employer to know about. This rule also applies to complaining about your employees, if you are the employer, and coworkers. If you have subordinates, address the problem directly.

Bad Date

A date can go downhill pretty fast if the people involved don't feel a love connection. Do not feel bad about not having a romantic interest in a person. If you have tried to get to know that person on two occasions, then break the news gently.

If the date is bad as a result of your doing, call the person and explain your shortcomings on the date. Nervousness is common and expected, so admit your nervousness and ask him out for a drink or coffee. This more casual meeting allows you to relax and show your personality more. If he declines your offer or does not return your call, it is his loss. Do not beat yourself up over it. There is someone else for you. When you are not on a date, go out and mingle with new people so you can relax and become more comfortable being yourself. You always have the option of hiring a dating coach. A coach can train you to be a great date and overcome your nerves.

Never Take a Bad Picture Again!

If you are notorious for ending up in candid photos with your mouth open, legs apart, and in some other horrible poses, use this technique to always get a great picture.

1. One certain thing is you must always *smile*. Smiling always brightens your look. Don't smile too big; this will only cause lines and make your eyes look small.

2. Find your pose and hold it. Avoid shifting and turning once you found your spot. It is almost certain that the camera will catch you between poses or blinking.

3. If you are standing, place one foot in front of the other at a ¾ angle, crossing your legs slightly. You can act as if you are taking a step to make the movement more casual instead of posing. Turn your upper body slightly so your shoulders are not squared straight to the camera. This position makes your body appear slim with slight curves. You can also have one leg out toward the side or the back and one hand on your hip. This pose elongates your legs and shows off a waist with confidence.

4. Always stand up straight with your shoulders back.

Tilt chin slightly down and look a little above the camera with your eyes.

Get to Know You Worksheet

In your own words, answer each question exactly the way you would if you were talking to a person. Using your own words allows you to express yourself freely and works your answers into your natural conversations without worrying about grammar (we normally write proper English and talk more casually).

Define yourself in one to two sentences.

What do you love most about yourself?

What is one thing you would like to change about yourself?

Describe the people you normally socialize with.

If you could spend the day doing anything you want, what would you do?

Who is your favorite author, and what is your favorite book? Why?

Which newspaper do you read the most? Why?

Who is your favorite musician, artist, or band?

Which museums do you like to visit?

Who is your favorite president? Why?

If you were to hold a public office, what position would that be? Why?

What is the most interesting place you've traveled to?

What country would you like to visit most? Why?

What is your favorite volunteer job? If you don't volunteer, what would you do to improve your community?

ACKNOWLEDGEMENTS

This book started after watching several women fighting on reality shows. So, I put pen to paper.

BIG thanks to my illustrator, Gloria Collazo. My words and ideas have been transformed into something relatable to everyone. She has worked so hard and supported me from day one.

Big thanks to Omar Tyree for the wonderful forward and guidance.

Thanks to Spelman College and Ansonia NAACP Youth Division for introducing me to etiquette.

Most of all I must thank my family and friends who took this journey with me.

My parents taught me to have standards and reminded me of my value throughout my young adult life. My mother proofed my book each step of the way. My father was always there to give me the male perspective. My sisters and brothers, Alita, Che, April, Ali, Carlitta, and Barbara helped guide the content. Lastly, thank you to my husband Yoji Cole or encouraging me every step of the way. Most of all, thank God for being in my heart and guiding my pen.

www.ingramcontent.com/pod-product-compliance
Lightning Source LLC
Chambersburg PA
CBHW060044030426
42334CB00019B/2481